LEARN GOLF
IN A WEEKEND

D0963031

LEARN GOLF IN A WEEKEND

PETER BALLINGALL

Photography by Matthew Ward

DORLING KINDERSLEY
London • New York • Sydney • Moscow
www.dk.com

A DORLING KINDERSLEY BOOK
www.dk.com

Art Editor Amanda Lunn
Series Editor James Harrison
Production Controller Meryl Silbert

First published in Great Britain in 1991
by Dorling Kindersley Limited,
9 Henrietta Street, London WC2E 8PS
First paperback edition published 1996

4 6 8 10 9 7 5

A CIP catalogue record for this book
is available from the British Library

ISBN 0-86318-595-9
ISBN 0-7513-0283-X Pbk

Computer page make-up by Cloud 9 Designs, Hampshire
Reproduced by Colourscan, Singapore
Printed and bound in Singapore
by KHL Printing Co Pte Ltd.

CONTENTS

INTRODUCTION

WELCOME TO THE WONDERFUL WORLD OF GOLF. The game
has been described as "the challenge of a life-time" – but you
have to start somewhere, and a well-structured weekend
course will set you up for the challenge. The aim of *Learn
Golf in a Weekend* is not just to teach you the basic golfing
techniques in a course lasting 12 hours over a weekend, but
also to show you that golf is very much a game of mental
approach whatever level of skill you reach.

Golf is not an easy game, but it is not so hard when all your
shots are made with ease. Understand the concepts that are
described in the following pages, and learn that it is not *how
you swing the club* but *what you do with the club face* that matters.

Use your imagination to picture yourself performing each skill successfully as you read through The Weekend Course. When you can see a sound swing in your mind's eye, and can get to know the feel of it, your progress will be assured. Once you understand the concepts and the basic principles described in this book, you will find that mental practice in the comfort of your armchair can be just as beneficial as doing the real thing.

Enjoy *Learn Golf in a Weekend* because even in a weekend you can grasp the gist of the game and understand those fundamentals which will guarantee your enjoyment.

PETER BALLINGALL

PREPARING FOR THE WEEKEND

Preparation is the key to a succcessful weekend

NOW YOU ARE COMMITTED to this weekend project try to find a practice partner – learning is easier this way. If you have played before, put previous concepts aside and study the skills afresh, paying particular attention to the words and phrases (many of which need to be reiterated for each skill). Choosing the right footwear and gloves will help your game. Perhaps the most important preparation for the course, and for further golfing enjoyment, is choosing the right clubs and balls. There can be few sports where the aerodynamics of the ball – the air flow, lift,

Air flow balls

Markers

ACCESSORIES

Pick up your essential pocket equipment and learn about golf ball types to suit your style of play (pp.14-15).

TEES

Plastic and wooden, long and short, take a varied selection of **tee pegs** for your weekend work-out (p.15).

Club loft and lie

5 wood	4 wood	3 wood	1 wood

Muscle memory exercises

FITNESS FACTORS

Get the feel of your swing muscles in action and memorize it (pp.20-21).

CLUBS

Learn about loft, length, angles and shafts (pp.10-13), and that golf is, above all, a game directed by the club face.

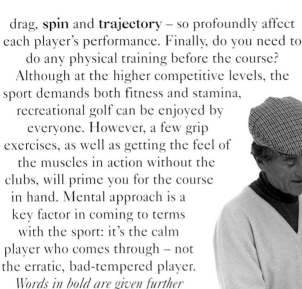

drag, **spin** and **trajectory** – so profoundly affect each player's performance. Finally, do you need to do any physical training before the course? Although at the higher competitive levels, the sport demands both fitness and stamina, recreational golf can be enjoyed by everyone. However, a few grip exercises, as well as getting the feel of the muscles in action without the clubs, will prime you for the course in hand. Mental approach is a key factor in coming to terms with the sport: it's the calm player who comes through – not the erratic, bad-tempered player.

Words in bold are given further explanation in the glossary (p.92).

THE COMPLETE GOLFER
Feel good in yourself and about the course.

BAGS
Whether you carry an extra light bag on your shoulders with half a dozen clubs, or take the full set in a tournament bag complete with caddy, choose only what you need and avoid the gimmicks.

DRESS SENSE
Wear clothes that allow you to stretch and swing, and that comply with standards of good taste.

GOLF CLUB DESIGN

From the distance drive to the shortest putt •

GOLF CLUBS ARE DIVIDED into **woods**, irons and **putters**. Woods – **drivers** and **fairway** woods – are designed for long distance shots; long, middle and short irons are for relative distance and accuracy; wedges (which are also irons) are designed for play out of long grass or sand; and putters, which come in all shapes and sizes, are for playing on the **greens**. You don't need the full set of 14 clubs – the maximum allowed on the course. Start off with a six club set, comprising a No 5 (**lofted**) wood; a 4-, a 6- and an 8-iron, a pitching wedge and a putter. Then, as you gain experience and are achieving more consistency of distance with these clubs, fill in the gaps with a **sand wedge**, a 9-, a 7-, a 5- and a 3-iron; a No 3 wood and, finally, the No 1 wood, or driver. Remember: lighter putters are suitable only for quick, dry greens.

• *Putter*

• *Iron*

• *Wood*

THE MAIN THREE CLUBS

The 3 essential clubs are a **driver** (metal or wood), middle distance iron and **putter**. Notice the difference in the length and design of each club.

ENSURE THE CORRECT FIT

FROM HANDLE TO HEEL

Every set of clubs, regardless of make or model, is made to conform to basic standards of length, lie and **loft**. If you are above- or below-average height, check with a golf pro (club professional) about getting the right lie and fit. Handle grips can be made thicker if you have large hands or stretched thinner for small hands.

CLUB LENGTH

If you are tall you will need extra length on the **shaft** and probably a more upright lie as well. Have the lie of each club adjusted to suit you. If you are shorter than average never have your clubs shortened because this will reduce your width of swing. This in turn will affect your natural club head speed and therefore your distance.

PUTTERS

A 1m (3ft) putt for the match can be the most difficult shot in golf. So have confidence in your putter and like it. Its design must please you, and its length and lie must suit you.

PUTTER SHAFTS •

Club shafts vary in length from roughly 86 – 94 cm (34 – 37 in), so make sure that the length of putter suits your posture. Never adjust your posture to suit the club. Ladies' clubs are lighter and shorter than men's, so youngsters can start with these.

SWEET SPOT MARKER

All putters have a sweet spot where the club's mass, or density, meets in the middle. When the ball contacts this area of the club face it rolls sweetly. A line or dot marks the spot.

FIND YOUR SWEET SPOT

Hold the club lightly with forefinger and thumb, letting the club hang freely. Tap along the blade with your other forefinger until the putter rebounds without twisting. This is the sweet spot.

HEEL & TOE

All clubs have a heel and a toe: the heel is at the near end and the toe at the far end of the club head.

Sweet spot •

Toe •

Heel •

Blade •

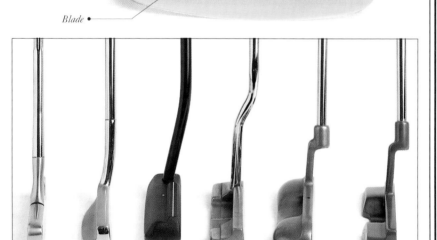

PUTTER DESIGNS

Putter shapes differ considerably. Many have a built-in design to ensure that the hands lead the **club head**. Weight also varies – heavier ones are for slower greens.

HANDLES

Putters usually have a flat-fronted handle allowing the thumbs to sit down the centre line (see p.27). Thick putter handles help to minimize any loose wrist action.

IRONS

There are two basic design variations in iron clubs – the classical **blade** and the peripheral weighted iron. The normal set of irons begins with a 3-iron and works through to the pitching and **sand wedges**. The 1- and 2-irons (otherwise known as driving irons, or "cleeks" in the early days) are for advanced players.

SHAFT LENGTH •
The length of the club **shaft** varies according to the **loft** of the **club face**. The less lofted clubs used for distance shots are longer than the lofted clubs used for accuracy. Each club gets progressively shorter by 12.5mm (¹/₂in) and each has an identification number on the **sole**.

Softer steel blade iron

GROOVES •
All irons have horizontal **grooves** across the **club face** to promote bite and **spin** for ball control.

CAVITY BACKED
In the peripheral-weighted or **cavity-backed** club the mass directly behind the hitting area is removed and disbursed around the edge of the club head. This expands the **sweet spot**, making it more "forgiving" and easy to use, and is therefore highly recommended for the inexperienced player.

TOE TIP
If it is possible to slip a coin under the club toe, at the address position, then the club is at the correct angle of lie.

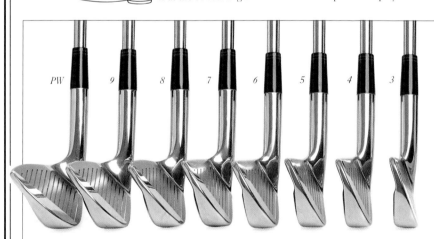

PW 9 8 7 6 5 4 3

LOOKING AT LOFT
You can see the increase in angle of loft from the 3-iron through to the pitching wedge. Each club is designed to make the ball react differently: the 3-iron is about 7cm (3in) longer than the pitching wedge, for example, so with the same amount of effort, a swing with a 3-iron will make the ball fly further with a lower **trajectory** than the pitching wedge.

WOODS

There are 2 basic types of **wood** design to choose from: "wood" woods and "metal" woods. Metal woods send the ball further and are less prone to damage.Woods are longer and less lofted than the driving iron and are designed for distance hitting, either from the **teeing ground** or from the **fairway**.

SHAFT-FLEX •

Club **shafts** range in flexibility from whippy to stiff. A regular flex of shaft is suitable for the average male, a more flexible shaft for the older golfer, and ladies' flex is tailor-made for women and youngsters. Only the stronger players get the true benefits of a stiff shaft.

• PW
• 5-iron
• No 3 wood

SOLE •

For technical reasons it is much more difficult – but not impossible – to alter the angle of **lie** of a wood. So all woods are made with a contour **sole** that should fit most standard-size golfers.

SWING PLANE

The longer the club the flatter it lies. Arranged in the manner above you can see that the length and **loft** determine the **plane** of the swing.

No 5 wood   *No 4 wood*   *No 3 wood*   *No 1 wood (driver)*

LEVEL OF LOFT

Woods come in various lengths and lofts and are numbered for identification: the higher the number, the greater the **loft** of each wood. Lofted woods are generally easier to play than long irons. Use any wood from the **teeing ground** and **fairway** (a No 5 wood propels the ball as far as a 3-iron). Only competition players attempt to use the No 1 off the grass.

GOLF ESSENTIALS

What you need to take with you around the golf course

GOLF IS A SPORT FULL OF GADGETS – some essential, others perhaps just design accessories of no material benefit in improving your game. The basic essentials covered here not only enable you to play, but also help you to leave the course in the condition in which you found it and so permit others to enjoy their game as well. You can buy them in all professional shops at golf courses or at retail sports outlets. Golf does require a considerable financial outlay, and obviously you have to budget for what you can afford; but once you have gathered together the equipment you need, you have covered a major outlay. Golf ball selection is just as critical to your game as choosing the right clubs – and ball aerodynamics vary greatly.

BALL DESIGN
Core, cover and compression, as well as **dimple** count, vary the ball's lift, drag and spin.

CHOOSING THE CORRECT BALL

BASIC BALL DESIGN
The wound 3-piece and the solid 2-piece are the two basic golf ball designs. The wound ball is more receptive to **spin** and is preferred by experienced players. Golf balls also differ by their compression – the measure of a ball's resistance to impact force. The options are 100 (high) or 90 (low) – 100 is harder, 90 softer.

THE INNER CORE
Hard-hitting players use a high compression ball with a soft balata (natural or synthetic rubber) cover for more receptive play. Average golfers should use the solid, more durable rubber core ball that spins less and rolls further. Lower 90 compression balls are best for beginners, as they optimize the feel of slower club head speed.

Wound 3-piece ball

Solid 2-piece ball

• TOWEL
Use golf towels
with special bag-
clips to keep
the club face
grooves free of
dirt.Clean your
golf balls before
teeing off.

SPONGER •
Dirt in the **dimples**
minimizes ball hitting
speed and distance, so wet
sponge the dirt out.

• MARKERS
On the **green** you
may lift and clean
your ball, but you
must mark the
exact spot where
it lay. Use a
marker or coin.

GRASS REPAIRERS •
When the ball lands on
the **green** from a great
height it creates an
indent mark on the
grass surface that must
be made good. Use a
pitchmark repairer to
smooth out the surface.

PRACTICE BALLS •
Plastic air-flow balls allow you the
flexibility to practise a full swing
in a relatively confined space.

• TEE PEGS
Graduated **tee pegs** set the right height from
the deep-faced driver to a lofted iron.
Plastic tees, though unbreakable, can
mark the plastic insert of woods.
Pros prefer wooden pegs.

• POCKET SIZE
The scorecard holder fits into
the pocket of the golf bag and
some even clip on to the trolley
handle for greater convenience.

GOLF KIT

Making the right selection to fit your needs

FOR GOLF CLUBS, bags, stands and trolleys go to the professional shop at a golf club. You can get on-the-spot expert advice on a wide selection of new and second-hand golf sets.

BEGINNER'S SET
A half set – comprising No 3 and No 5 **woods**, 4-, 6- and 8-**irons**, **pitching wedge** and **putter** – is ideal to begin with. A lightweight golf bag completes your set.

INTERMEDIATE SET
As you progress, add to your set. Make sure that you will be able to add matching clubs to your set as your playing improves.

• CLUB COVERS
Synthetic club-head covers provide all-weather protection as well as preventing scuffing in the bag.

• WOODS
You get more distance off the metal-face **woods** than off the plastic insert face of true woods. Metal-face woods also need less looking after.

• TOWEL
Ensure there is nothing on the club face that might deflect your next shot.

SUPPORT •
Keep your clubs and bag off wet or muddy ground with a bag stand.

UMBRELLA •
Indispensable for wet weather, and a useful practice aid (see p.86).

THE PROFESSIONAL SET
A professional bag with a full set of clubs, plus accessories and all the wet-weather gear in the pockets, is too heavy to carry over 18 holes (unless you have a caddy), so a sturdy and manoeuvrable trolley is essential.

COVERS •
There are a variety of hood covers designed to protect clubs against the elements, as well as to prevent club wear and tear when travelling.

• TRAVEL BAGS
Golf hold-alls contain a zipped section to separate dirty golf shoes from shirts, slacks and socks.

• TROLLEYS
Look for an easy-folding trolley with quick-release straps and wide wheels for good stability.

GOLF CLOTHES

What to wear and when to wear it

GOLFERS ARE INFLUENCED by what the pros wear and golf club shops are full of bright coloured short-sleeved shirts, polo neck or V-neck sweaters and check or plain trousers. The more flamboyant the personality the more colourful the attire? Perhaps, but there is a basic standard of dress that requires men to wear shirts with sleeves and collars and tailored trousers – no tracksuits, denim jeans or singlets. Golf is an all-weather game which is reflected by the clothes and accessories shown below.

FROM HEAD TO TOE

Comfort is the key to a good golf swing, so in hot or cold weather, be it dry or damp, these useful golf accessories will help keep out the elements.

MITTENS •
If your hands are cold you can't get a decent grip and you won't be able to play good golf. In cold weather put on golf mittens such as these between shots.

GLOVES •
Golf gloves act as a second skin to improve the adhesion of the grip even when holding the club lightly. Use an all-weather glove in wet weather and a thin leather type for normal play.

BOOTS •
Specially-designed golf boots are a sensible option if you really want to keep out the rain.

A SURE FOOT •
Ribbed and pebble soles give a reasonable tread, but serious players wear spike-studded soles for a secure swing footing.

HEADWEAR •
Both wind in your hair and sun in your eyes detract from making good golf shots. A woollen hat or sun visor will help solve these problems.

HEAD SENSE •
Acrylic or wool caps or hats keep your head warm and your vision unhindered.

NO SWEAT •
Modern synthetic, breathable fabrics prevent excessive perspiration (unlike nylon lining) but at a price. The raglan sleeve permits free movement and many models have air vents to release inside moisture.

CARE •
Always hang dry your waterproofs after each game. They will serve you better and last longer.

WET-WEATHER GEAR

Waterproof jackets should be light and roomy and, ideally, rustle-free. At the cheap end of the market come the nylon showerproof variety of wet-weather gear. The 100% waterproof breathable fabrics cost a lot more, but are worth it as they are resistant to wind and rain.

• UMBRELLA
Golf umbrellas come in 3 main sizes – the pro size naturally is the largest.

SMART PLAY
Comfort is the key to summer play – give yourself room to manoeuvre and always carry a light pullover as well as light windcheater in case the weather takes a turn for the worse – after all, you may be out on the course for many hours.

FIT FOR GOLF

Muscle movement and memory: exercise for mind and body

WALKING IS ONE OF THE BEST WAYS of exercising the body's muscles, and on an 18-hole course you can expect to walk some 6 km (4 miles) up hill and down dale carrying or pulling a bag of clubs. So you build up fitness as you play the game. While golf does not require the muscle-building exercises of more gruelling sports, upper body stretches will help your swing action, and a tyre-drill routine strengthens wrists and forearms.

• SHOULDERS
Keep the shoulder and back muscles completely relaxed. Exercise only the hand and forearm muscles.

WRIST STRENGTHENING

A car tyre and a squash, or rubber, ball provide two useful props for golf grip and swing exercises. Using both in the manner decribed here will help strengthen your wrist muscles.

PALM PRESSURE
Hold a soft ball in your hand – palm upwards. Squeeze the ball with your fingers and relax. Go on until you begin to feel the pressure come into the forearm. Now swop hands.

• WRIST
Strong wrists mean more efficient play and, ideally, your left- and right-hand wrists should be of equal strength.

WRIST BUILD-UP
Cup the wrists when doing this routine for extra muscle tension and stop when you feel the pressure. Don't overdo fitness drills as this may lead to muscle strain.

PRACTICE
Start with a 20- to 30-second routine with each hand, then build up the session lengths gradually and practise the drill more often.

• ACTION
Hold any club one-handed by the club head and place the handle inside an old tyre rim. Move the wrists so that the club handle hits opposite sides of the upper rim in turn. Start off slowly at first, then speed up the exercise.

MUSCLE MEMORY

Before you play, practise the full golf swing without a golf club to create the necessary muscle memory for the correct movements of the swing.

STANCE •
The golf swing should be an effortless interaction of body movements (see pp.50-55). Rotate your body from the **address** position as shown to get the feel of the muscles.

• PALMS
Placing the hands back-to-back helps to produce the feel of a golf swing without having to hold a club. An imaginary golf hand grip will also do.

TURN BACK
As you lean over from the hips rotate the upper body to the right letting the hips, legs and feet respond in sympathy.

TURN THROUGH
As the weight transfers to the left side, the hips rotate and the right foot ends up on the toes, with the heel completely off the ground.

MORE MUSCLE MEMORY EXERCISES

REVOLVING CENTRE SWING
Stand with hands on hips in an **address** position. Transfer all your weight to your left foot (for right-handers). Put all your weight on the left side. Rotate the knees, hips, chest, torso and eyes to face to the left in that order. Hold the position and raise the back foot off the ground to ensure that all of your weight is correctly transferred. The feeling is of turning to the left easily without any body restrictions.

INDEPENDENT ARM SWING
To feel "dis-connected" from the shoulders hold each arm straight out and let them free-fall so hands slap thighs.

MIRROR IMAGE MARKING
Swing the arms and hands around and up to the right in front of a mirror. Watch the reactions of the body and feel what happens. Swing them back again and up to the other side. Observe the reaction of the body. Make a mark on the mirror where your head is reflected and perform the exercise without moving off the mark.

ACHIEVING A LOW GRAVITY
You need a low centre of gravity so practise feeling heavy. Stand in front of a mirror and reach for the sky. Stretch high, poised like a ballerina, then relax and feel your weight sink, poised like a wrestler in the ring.

THE WEEKEND COURSE

Understanding the course at a glance

THE COURSE COVERS TEN SKILLS, divided into two days of practice. Starting with how to hold the clubs on pp.24-27, move on to learn about **stance**, **address** and **posture** (pp.28-31). How to putt, chip, pitch and play the full swing are also covered on Day 1. The second day is devoted to ball control, bunker shots, playing awkward lies and how to play a par-4 hole. You will progress faster when you familiarize yourself with the different aspects of the golf course and try to understand what the course designer is asking of you. Relate this also to your scorecard and playing ability (see pp.78-83, 88-89).

The take away or backswing

DAY 1		Hours	Page
SKILL 1	Golf Grips	¹/2	24-27
SKILL 2	Setting Up	¹/2	28-31
SKILL 3	Putting	1	32-37
SKILL 4	Chipping	1	38-43
SKILL 5	Pitching	1	44-49
SKILL 6	Full Swing	2	50-55

Chipping

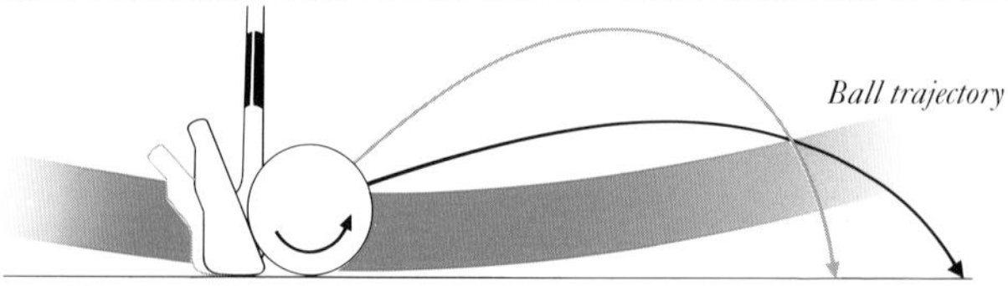

Ball trajectory

KEY TO SYMBOLS

CLOCKS

Small clocks appear on the first page of each new skill. They highlight, through the blue coloured section, how long you might spend on that skill and show where the skill fits in your day. For example, check the clock on p.28. The blue segment shows that ½ hour should be set aside for Skill 2: Setting Up, and the grey section shows that ½ hour was spent on the previous skill. But be flexible, use clocks as guidelines only, and settle in to a natural pace.

RATING SYSTEM •••••

Each skill is given a star rating according to the degree of difficulty. One bullet (•) denotes that the skill is comparatively straightforward, while 5 bullets (•••••) are given to the most challenging skills.

MICRO-MEN

The series of micro-men, alongside each playing skill, shows the number of steps involved for each skill. The blue coloured men identify the steps which are illustrated.

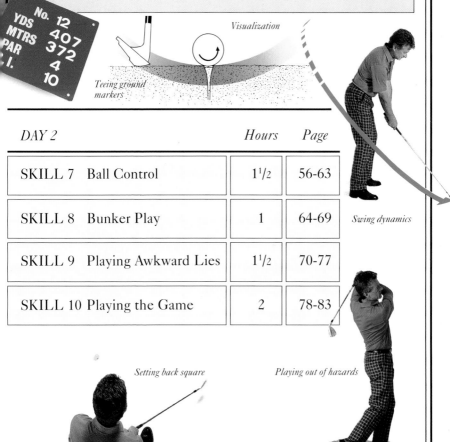

Visualization

Teeing ground markers

No. 12
YDS 407
MTRS 372
PAR 4
I. 10

Swing dynamics

Setting back square

Playing out of hazards

DAY 2		Hours	Page
SKILL 7	Ball Control	1½	56-63
SKILL 8	Bunker Play	1	64-69
SKILL 9	Playing Awkward Lies	1½	70-77
SKILL 10	Playing the Game	2	78-83

1

GOLF GRIPS

Definition: *Alternative ways of holding the club*

GRIP IS AN UNFORTUNATE WORD because it suggests "tight", and golf is a game of feel – a game played with elasticity of movement rather than physical strength. There are several different holds you can adopt, depending on the strength or weakness of your grip.

OBJECTIVE: To think of your hands as sensors. *Rating* •••••

THE VARDON GRIP

This overlapping grip is the most widely used for holding the club securely, and is best for all golfers, except those with small hands.

1 Place the golf-club handle diagonally across the left hand, so it rests from the heel along the palm to the forefinger.

2 Sit the club in the crook of the forefinger, which acts as a trigger finger. Now wrap the fingers around the handle for a secure hold.

GOLFER'S VIEW
The thumb sits slightly to the right, and has a light purchase on the handle as does the forefinger.

PISTOL-GRIP •
Make a pistol-like grip with 3 fingers around the butt, placing the forefinger through the "trigger loop" and thumb just to the right of the "hammer".

"V" SHAPE •
The "V" shape formed by the forefinger and thumb points towards your right ear.

3 Position the club handle in the crook of the middle two fingers of the right hand – not down in the base of the fingers.

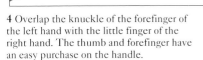

4 Overlap the knuckle of the forefinger of the left hand with the little finger of the right hand. The thumb and forefinger have an easy purchase on the handle.

OVERLAP GRIP

The **Vardon grip** has the little finger of the right hand overlapping the left forefinger knuckle .The last 3 fingers of the left hand are firm but without tension. Feel each finger on the handle; they act as sensors.The right feel is between tight and tense, and sloppy and light.

WRISTS •
The wrists should feel firm but not rigid. Being hinges, they respond to the actions of the body and the arms.

• SHAFT
Remember your grip directs both the angle of the club **shaft** to club **face** to ball, as well as the angle of your arms and **address** position.

• RIGHT THUMB
Sit the right thumb slightly to the left of the centre line of the handle so that it has a purchase with the forefinger.

• "V" SHAPE
The "V" formed by thumb and forefinger points towards the right shoulder.

SKILL

1

GETTING TO GRIPS

Although a text-book grip is desirable, many golfers hold the club in an individual way to compensate for their style of swing. In any event a light hold is crucial.

VARDON GRIP
Named after its inventor, Harry Vardon, this over-lapping grip has become the recommended text-book method for holding the club lightly but securely.

INTERLOCKING GRIP
If you have small or weak hands try the interlocking grip. Instead of overlapping the little finger of the right hand with the forefinger of the left, interlock them.

BASEBALL GRIP
Adults with small hands, as well as youngsters, should try the baseball, or two-handed, grip, where all 8 fingers are on the handle. Both palms face each other.

GETTING IT JUST RIGHT

SUIT YOUR STYLE
Go for the grip that suits you best but always hold the club lightly. The key is neither to hold the handle in the palm, nor in the base of the fingers, but somewhere between the two. Bear in mind that when you hold the club, the **club face** does whatever your hands do.

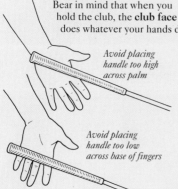

Avoid placing handle too high across palm

Avoid placing handle too low across base of fingers

GRIP TEST
Suspend the club in the heel of your hand and last three fingers . Hold the handle lightly but securely enough to feel the weight of the **club head**.

GRIP CHECKLIST
1 Make sure the club is sitting in the heel of left hand.
2 Have no more than 2 knuckles showing.
3 The left thumb is encased by right pad.
4 The club sits in the crook of the middle fingers of the right hand.
5 Feel the hold of the right forefinger and right thumb.
6 Feel each finger in position.

THE PUTTING GRIP

You'll need to adopt a special grip when putting to reduce wrist action and increase control of the **club face**.

1 Set the putter on the ground, and place the last 3 fingers of the left hand and the first 3 fingers of the right hand on the handle. Both thumbs are off the handle at this stage.

2 While keeping the fingers close together, position the left thumb down the centre, then the right thumb on top. Keep the grip light, but secure.

PUTTER FINGERS
Allow both the forefinger as well as the little finger to overlap the putter handle as illustrated.

PUTTER HANDLE •
Almost all putters have a specially designed flat top surface to accomodate the thumb positions as shown.

• CLUB SHAFT
Ensure the **club head** is set correctly on the ground by arching the wrists and forcing the club **shaft** downwards. This also sets the wrists firmly.

THUMB •
Sit the right thumb pad over the left thumb, facing directly down the putter handle and **shaft**.

BUTT •
Leave at least 1cm ($1/4$in) of the putter handle showing to give you the right depth of grip.

SKILL

2

SETTING UP

Definition: *Addressing the ball with the club face and aligning yourself to the target with the correct club for the distance*

MOST GOLF ERRORS occur as you are setting up and addressing the ball – before the swing even begins – so bear in mind the following points. **1** The ball always travels in line with the angle of the **club face** at impact, therefore align the club face directly to the target. **2** The alignment of your body determines the direction of the **swing path**. **3** Your posture dictates the **swing plane**.

OBJECTIVE: To achieve the best body posture and club face alignment for the intended shot. *Rating* •••••

Step 1

TAKE UP YOUR TARGET

Before attempting to play any shot first consider all your options – your lie, length of shot, terrain, hazards and so on – then visualize the shot turning out successfully. This is known as **target orientating**.

• **THINK VISUAL**
When setting up think where to send the ball rather than how to swing the club.

• **BODY-TO-CLUB**
Although the club is relatively light it increases in weight once the swing gets underway. So position the body around the club and ball so that you can transfer your weight and turn easily in a perfectly balanced state.

HOLD •
Hold your arms out in front as your hands grip the handle.

LOWER TORSO •
Keep the lower body relaxed at this stage.

GRIP
Hold the club lightly using the **Vardon grip** (see pp.24-25), or the baseball (two-handed) grip if your hands are small (pp.26-27).

RIGHT FOOT •
Keeping both hands on the handle lean over with the right foot leading as you prepare to place the club in position behind the ball.

• **BALL**
Concentrate on sending the ball easily to its target. Feel that what you are about to do is easy; don't become mesmerized by the ball.

Step 2

AIMING

Align the **club face** carefully so that its bottom edge is square to the target. The top edge shows you the upward path into which you will be swinging the club. This alters from club to club depending on the **loft**, length and angle of **shaft**.

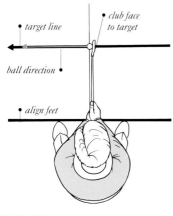

target line

club face to target

ball direction

align feet

• GOLFER'S VIEW
Before attempting to play any shot, you must first consider all your options. Then try to see the successful result in your mind's eye.

• BODY-TO-BALL
Place the club into position by keeping both hands on the handle; this should automatically give you the correct distance of stance from the ball. Many poor shots result from a poor positioning, where the golfer stands either too close or too far away from the ball.

• CLUB FACE
Remember it's not you hitting the ball, it's the **club face**; so aim the face carefully with the bottom edge square to the target to achieve the correct impact.

STANCE
Once you are satisfied that you have placed the club in the correct position, then you should realign your feet (as shown above) so that the tips of your toes align in a direction parallel to the line from the ball to the target.

ALIGNMENT TO TARGET

DOWN THE TRACK
The imaginary guidelines shown here in front of the toes, hips and shoulders do not go to the target – they run parallel with the imaginary line that runs through the ball and goes to the target. Try visualizing the ball sitting on one line of a railway track which goes to the target, while you stand on the other line – this gives you the proper perspective. Railway lines appear to meet on the horizon (but don't), so you must align your body to a point just to the left of target.

AIMING TIP
To sight the **club face** accurately, line it up to a marker only a metre or so in front of the ball – in line with the ultimate target.

SKILL

2

ALIGNMENT

Align your body at right angles to the **bottom edge** of the club (now placed behind the ball). Your body **alignment** dictates the direction in which the club swings, so be sure that the lines across your shoulders, hips and toes are parallel to the target line.

SHOULDER •
As the right hand sits lower on the handle than the left, so the right shoulder is lower than the left one. Let both shoulders hang down limply to eliminate tension.

HANDS •
Keep the hands over the ball.

WEIGHT DISTRIBUTION •
The dotted lines indicate how evenly the body weight is distributed for medium irons. When using **woods** off the tee, and also long fairway clubs, keep your weight approximately 60 per cent in favour of the right side. For short, very lofted, clubs shift your weight 60 per cent in favour of the left.

• ELBOWS AND ARMS
The elbows point towards the hips rather than outwards. The left arm is comfortably straight and the right one slightly bent and relaxed.

LINING UP
With short and middle range clubs, there is a relatively straight line from the left shoulder down the left arm to the shaft and **club head**.

• FEET
Make sure both feet are pointed outwards – the left one facing at 11 o'clock, and the right facing at 1 o'clock. This more easily enables the upper body to turn fully in the backwards swing, and the lower to rotate through to the target in a well balanced fashion.

BALL-TO-STANCE POSITION

WHERE TO PLAY THE BALL
Tournament professionals may favour playing the ball from just inside the left heel, but as a beginner let the design of the club influence the position of the ball in relation to your stance. The illustration shows clearly that for the club face of a driver (the longest club) to look at the target, you must play the ball from just inside the instep or heel of the left foot. Similarly a medium iron such as a 5- or 6-iron will look at the target when you place it mid-way between centre of stance and the left heel. When using a lofted club, such as a pitching wedge or sand iron, the design suggests that you should position the ball in centre of stance so that the club face looks directly at the target.

ESTABLISHING A GOOD POSTURE

DOING THE GROUNDWORK

The setting up steps are hold it (the club), aim it (the **club face**), and face it (the bottom edge of the club face). Now you must establish a good posture. This lays the foundations for the following.

• A rotation of the body in the backward and forward movements in a state of perfect balance.

• Freedom for the arms to swing up and down on a correct plane in accordance with the club you've selected.

FIRE FROM THE HIPS

Good golfers stand tall to the ball and lean over from the hips – never the waist. This allows the spine to remain relatively straight so that it can rotate easily. The knees are slightly flexed and the arms and hands hang comfortably downwards.

PERMANENT ADDRESS

This side-on view shows how the golfer's posture hardly changes for any of the golf clubs being used to address the ball.

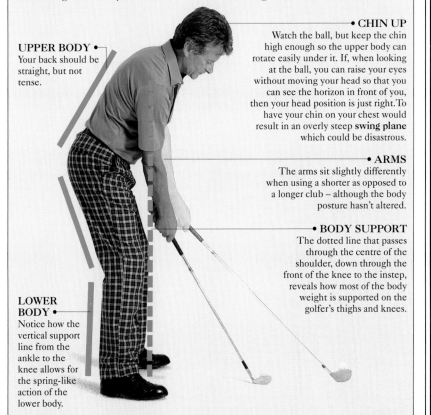

UPPER BODY •
Your back should be straight, but not tense.

• CHIN UP
Watch the ball, but keep the chin high enough so the upper body can rotate easily under it. If, when looking at the ball, you can raise your eyes without moving your head so that you can see the horizon in front of you, then your head position is just right. To have your chin on your chest would result in an overly steep **swing plane** which could be disastrous.

• ARMS
The arms sit slightly differently when using a shorter as opposed to a longer club – although the body posture hasn't altered.

• BODY SUPPORT
The dotted line that passes through the centre of the shoulder, down through the front of the knee to the instep, reveals how most of the body weight is supported on the golfer's thighs and knees.

LOWER BODY •
Notice how the vertical support line from the ankle to the knee allows for the spring-like action of the lower body.

SKILL

3

PUTTING

Definition: *The final act of holing out, of sinking the ball in the hole*

PUTTING REQUIRES A smoothness of movement, a firm resolve and commitment, a feel for pace and a positive visualization that the ball will go in the hole. Many great players fade away not because they can no longer strike the golf ball well, but because they lose their nerve on the **greens**. Sometimes this is due to a suspect technique but the main fault is an underlying mistrust and doubt about themselves. Putt compactly, that is, with no "melting" or flicking of the wrists.

OBJECTIVE: To make solid contact and ensure that the putter faces and travels on its predetermined path. *Rating* •••••

READING THE GREEN

PRIMARY TARGET

Few putting **greens** are absolutely flat, but every putt is a straight putt – straight that is, to a point on the green after which the contour or slope causes the ball to break to the left or right. Stand back from the ball and assess the slope's severity, picking a **primary target** for the ball to reach before the ball's roll is affected by the contour.

PUTTING DOWNHILL

Downhill putts on fast greens can lead to a nervous tentative action. The best way of dealing with these shots is to play the ball off the **toe** or the **heel** of the putter. Every putter has a **sweet spot** towards the centre of the **club face** (see p.11). Hit the ball away from this point and the ball leaves the putter "dead" and does not race away.

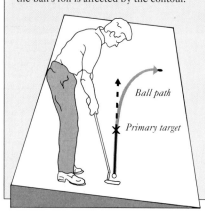

Ball path

Primary target

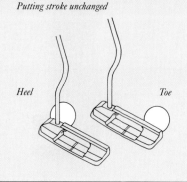

Putting stroke unchanged

Heel

Toe

Step 1

ADDRESS

Stand tall and lean over from the hips. Flex the knees. Avoid tension by letting the shoulders, arms and hands hang comfortably. Stand with feet about shoulder-width apart and feel balanced in a state of relaxed readiness.

HEAD •
If the shoulders are relaxed the head will remain still. But don't let it hang too low or your movements will be cramped and awkward.

SHOULDERS •
Notice the right shoulder sits a little lower than the left. Ensure that the line across the shoulders is parallel to the **target line**.

ARMS •
Let your arms hang comfortably. Feel the light connection of your upper arms to your body as though holding a towel under the armpits.

ELBOWS •
Point the elbows more inwards towards each hip rather than outwards.

WRISTS •
Arch the wrists as though forcing the putter head downwards. This sets them securely.

HANDS •
Settle the hands slightly forward of the putter head. Adopt the putter grip (see p.27).

FEET •
Keep your feet shoulder-width apart, and align them parallel to the **target line**.

CORRECT POSTURE
Keep the lower back straight after leaning over from the hips, with wrists arched and eyes looking directly over the ball.

CLUB HEAD-TO-BALL
Many players prefer to suspend the putter head fractionally above the ground at address. Others let it rest lightly on the ground.

• KNEES
Flex the knees slightly and relax them. As you are still and quiet in the upper body feel that your knees and feet are bearing your body weight. Feel the ground coming up into your soles.

• BALL
Position yourself to the ball somewhere between the centre of your stance and left heel.

SKILL

3

Step 2

TAKE AWAY

The **back swing** is a smooth one-piece step in which the action of the upper body and arms influences the movement of the club head. Throughout the back swing, or take away, the lower body is still.

HEAD •
The head is the hub of the arc of swing, as shown fully in sequence on pp.36-37. If the head moves off its axis your putting will be inconsistent.

UPPER BODY •
Keep the triangle of shoulders-to-arms-to-hands in a smooth rocking action rather like a pendulum, as the left shoulder comes down a little and the right one goes up.

ARMS •
The arms move in sympathy with the body. There is no tightness or tension and the angles are all unaltered from the position held at address.

GRIP •
Maintain a firm hold on the handle and keep the wrists arched to ensure that no bending inwards take place. The left wrist is flat (straight) and remains this way throughout the stroke. The right wrist has a slight kink and remains this way also.

CLUB HEAD •
Poor results occur when the club is picked up too early in the take away. Keep the **club head** close to the ground in the back swing and the correct geometry will follow.

• OBSERVE
Without moving your eyes simply observe the putter face moving away from, and through the ball, and experience the smoothness of that movement. Notice that the club face appears to fan open a little – but it doesn't because the hands and wrists are doing nothing. So the eyes should simply observe the action. Unfortunately, we tend to attach judgements to what we see and, therefore, feel that we "have to do". This can place doubts in the mind and affect the performance.

• HIPS
Keep your hips comfortably still. Be sure that the pelvic area is down and back so as to keep the lower back straight. Correct posture is vital and this should be rehearsed often in front of a mirror. If the hips remain still so too will the knees and legs, creating a steady base for the action of the swing.

Target line   *Ball position*

Swing path

Stance

SWING PATH
The putter's **swing path** tracks away from the ball (keeping close to the ground) in a slight arc – not in a straight line away from the target. On the forward swing the putter faces and travels straight through to the target.

• BALL
Think of the ball as lying in the way of your swing, rather than how to hit it.

LEARNING ABOUT DISTANCES

FEEL FOR PACE

Most people imagine that the direction of the putt is its most important aspect, but **pace** is the critical factor. More second putts are missed because the first one has been struck too softly or firmly rather than because it was too wide of the target. Learn the feel for pace. Roll the ball underarm to any preselected target. How much back swing did it take to roll it that far? Now make a putt in the same manner.

PUTTING SKILL DRILLS

1 For 10 minutes only practise putting to a hole (or a mug on the carpet) with your eyes closed. After each putt, and before opening your eyes, try to gauge by feel whether the ball was short or long, left or right. Learn to get the feel of the shot.

2 For 10 minutes putt alternately to 2 targets of varying length. For the longer putts simply aim to stop the ball within a "dustbin lid" of the hole.

Step 3

,THE STROKE

Concentrate on the total movement where one third is on the backward swing and two thirds on the forward one. This will ensure that even on shorter putts the putter head is accelerating through impact.

• THINK TRIANGLES
Notice that the shoulders have rocked back again and that the triangle of shoulders-to-arms-to-hands is still intact. The arms, hands and putter just come along for the ride, maintaining a compact uniformity. The position of the body at impact has returned to its original **address** position.

• HANDS
Notice how the hands lead the **club head**, and how the putter follows behind the body's swing movement.

• WEIGHT
Because the ball is positioned slightly to the left of centre, the body weight also favours the left side – but avoid leaning over too far to the left.

• SUPPORT
Keep the feet, legs and hips steady, avoiding any rigidity or tension.

FOLLOW THROUGH
Many putts are missed because the player looks up too early. This causes the upper body's pendulum movement to change direction. So listen for the contact first, then look.

SKILL

3

PUTTING IN ACTION

We all see and feel things in different ways, but notice in the putting sequence the three essential qualities of a good putting stroke: **1** The triangle created by the shoulder line and arms never alters. **2** The ratio of the swing is one third back and two thirds through. **3** The wrists and hands remain "set" throughout – there is no flick of the wrists.

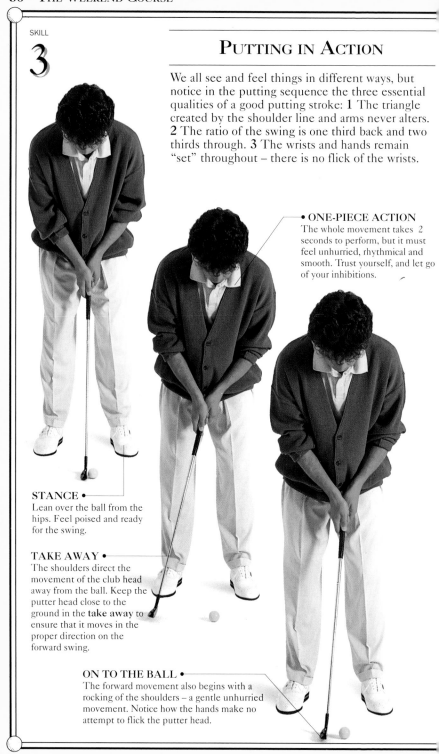

• ONE-PIECE ACTION
The whole movement takes 2 seconds to perform, but it must feel unhurried, rhythmical and smooth. Trust yourself, and let go of your inhibitions.

STANCE •
Lean over the ball from the hips. Feel poised and ready for the swing.

TAKE AWAY •
The shoulders direct the movement of the club head away from the ball. Keep the putter head close to the ground in the **take away** to ensure that it moves in the proper direction on the forward swing.

ON TO THE BALL •
The forward movement also begins with a rocking of the shoulders – a gentle unhurried movement. Notice how the hands make no attempt to flick the putter head.

SWING THOUGHTS

THE MENTAL APPROACH

Put yourself through the mental game to help you get the feel of the swing. Repeat the actions often in front of a mirror so that you are able to relate the feel to the image. See the stroke clearly in your mind's eye. The body achieves what the mind perceives.

FREE FLOWING

Allow your natural body movement to play its part. On any golf shot the good golfer feels his swing as a continuous action, where the senses control the shot. The golfer should try always to keep the stroke as smooth as possible.

MIND'S EYE IMAGE

Build a clear picture of what you want your body to do then let it happen. Don't over-concentrate on the hit; trust yourself and let go of your inhibitions.

A PUTT MISSED

Don't be frightened of missing. If you have mis-judged the pace of the putt, let your senses correct the next shot – but always aim for a smooth stroke.

• CONSISTENCY
Notice the shoulders-to-arms-to-hands triangle keeps moving unaltered, unchanged.

• FOLLOW THROUGH
Looking up too soon breaks the rhythm of a good golf shot. On shorter putts listen, then look.

BALL CONTROL•
The face of the putter is looking at, and moving towards, the target. Logic demands that the ball must go there too.

SKILL

4 CHIPPING

DAY 1

Definition: *A stroke played within about 3.5m (12ft) of the putting surface*

CHIPPING IS PUTTING ... with a **lofted** putter. Use a 4-, 6-, or 8-iron or **wedge**, or a 3-, 5-, 7-, or 9-iron for this shot, depending on how high the ball must fly or how far it must roll.

OBJECTIVE: To carry the ball over rougher grass so it lands on the green and rolls like a putt to the hole. *Rating* •••

Step 1

ADDRESS

Take up the same **address** position as you would for the **putting** stroke (see p.32), but use a 7- or 8-iron instead.

SHOULDERS
Align the shoulders parallel to the **target line**. Notice that the right shoulder sits lower than the left.

SPOT ON
Focus on a spot a few centimetres past the ball.

GRIP
Place hands down the handle to putter's length regardless of the club you choose. This brings you as close to the ball as for putting. Arch the wrists; this brings the heel of the club off the surface, so that the club sits on its toe and you avoid scuffing the ground.

HIPS
Notice the angle of the belt line. The hips and bottom are back, out of the way, creating a counterbalance to the head which is over the ball.

KNEES
Flex the knees comfortably.

FEET
Place the feet about shoulder-width apart with weight mainly on the left foot.

BALL
Place the ball at centre or left of centre of your stance.

THE RIGHT ANGLE
Good posture is vital: spine to hips, hips to knees, knees to feet are all straight lines and angles – no curves.

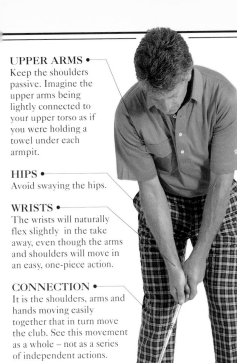

UPPER ARMS •
Keep the shoulders
passive. Imagine the
upper arms being
lightly connected to
your upper torso as if
you were holding a
towel under each
armpit.

HIPS •
Avoid swaying the hips.

WRISTS •
The wrists will naturally
flex slightly in the take
away, even though the arms
and shoulders will move in
an easy, one-piece action.

CONNECTION •
It is the shoulders, arms and
hands moving easily
together that in turn move
the club. See this movement
as a whole – not as a series
of independent actions.

Step 2
TAKE AWAY

As you take away
your chosen
chipping club, see
and look at the ball
but feel the rhythm and ease of
the swing movement.

Target line

Swing plane

Body alignment

ARC OF THE SWING
The club tracks away from the
target line in the take away. See
the **club face** return on the same
arc at impact and follow through
straight to the target.

FINDING THE RIGHT FLIGHT PATH

BALL SPIN
More **loft** equals more back spin and height.
Swing down and through, never under and
up. The club should return on the same
swing path as in the take away.

AIM
When chipping to the **green**, aim at a
primary target that is in line with the hole
– not the hole itself. It is easier to line up
on something less than a metre or so away.

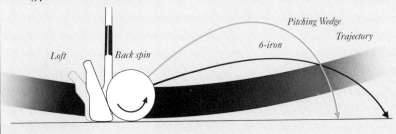

Pitching Wedge

Trajectory

6-iron

Loft   *Back spin*

SKILL

4

Step 4
THE HIT

Feel the contact as part of the total swing movement rather than a single action. Visualize the triangle formed by the shoulder line and arms as unchanging.

• HEAD STEADY
Observe the **club face** as it passes through the ball, and keep the head steady.

• UPPER ARMS
Move the shoulders and arms together; they should feel lightly connected to the upper torso.

• HIP TURN
Rotate the hips in sympathy – like a door opening for the arms to pass through freely.

• WRIST ACTION
Keep the left wrist straight, leading the **club face**. Keep the right wrist cocked.

• ORDER OF PLAY
The sequence of your swing is: body, then arms and lastly the **club head**.

• CONSTANT SWING
The ball lies in the way of the movement: let the club swing through the ball. Its **loft** will make the ball rise and roll.

FORWARD IMPACT
You've made contact and the ball is on its way. The **club face** should still be moving forwards, towards the hole too, even after impact.

CHIPPING TIPS

CHIPPING PRACTICE
Stand about 2m (6ft 6in) from the edge of a putting **green** and aim to land the ball inside a ring of **tee pegs** roughly 1m (3ft) on to the putting surface. Notice the distance each ball rolls upon landing using an 8- and 6-iron and pitching wedge in turn.

BRUSH THE GRASS
As you swing through the target, simply brush through the grass. The more you get used to the feel of the shot the easier it will become for you to select the correct club to give you the right amount of roll for the distance needed.

Pitching wedge   *8-iron*   *6-iron*

Step 5

FOLLOW THROUGH

The take away, or take back, accounts for one-third of the total swing, while the follow through, or through swing, takes up two-thirds just as in a tennis swing or bowling action. The easiest way to get the ball up is to try to keep the ball down in the through swing.

SWING AXIS
Your head is the hub of the swing – the central axis around which all other parts rotate. Keep your chin up, literally. Watch the contact and then observe the flight and roll of the ball.

UPPER BODY
Think of your shoulders and arms as a triangle that should be kept intact as your upper body moves easily like a pendulum. Try to keep the shoulders relaxed and free of tension.

HIPS
Rotate the hips slightly like a door opening, allowing the arms, hands and club head to pass through.

KNEES
The right knee responds to the action of the hips by moving towards the target.

FEET
As the right knee moves towards the target, the right heel comes slightly off the ground.

EYES DOWN
Looking up too early can ruin your shot, so listen first then look. The sound of the contact of iron with ball can tell you how "sweet" the shot is on impact. If your rhythm is smooth then your shot should flow well too.

UPPER ARMS
The upper arms begin to lose their connection with the body as they direct the **club face** towards the target after impact.

NO WRIST ACTION
Hands and wrists do nothing. The left wrist remains straight – and arched – while the right wrist stays cocked exactly as in the take away. There must be no flexing of the wrists.

CLUB
Think of the **club head** as the last part of the sequence – body, then arms and lastly the club head. The **club face** should still face the target after impact.

LOFT
The ball reacts with the **club face**, flying and rolling depending on how much loft is on the club face, so choice of club is paramount.

SKILL
4

CHIPPING IN ACTION

Observe the chipping sequence as a whole movement rather than as isolated actions. Visualize the gentle rocking action of the torso and shoulders, and notice how the triangle of shoulders and arms is maintained throughout. The movement of this triangle – not the wrists or hands – sets up the movement of the club head.

• HANDS
The hands always lead the club head: never let the club head pass the hands by attempting to scoop the ball.

POISED •
Feel relaxed and ready with the shoulders, arms and hands passive, but the wrists arched and set to stay immobile.

STEADY •
Feel steady in the **take away** and avoid any flick of the wrist. Look for a smooth one-piece action of arms and upper body.

RESPOND •
Don't rush the **club head** in to the ball. Let it lag behind and it will come back at the right time and speed, if your hands and arms simply respond to the gentle rocking of the shoulders.

SWING THOUGHTS

- One third back and two thirds through makes for correct contact on the ball.
- One constant stroke from no more than 3m (10ft) off the green will land the ball about 1m (3ft) on to the putting surface.
- Club selection depends upon the amount of roll required to take the ball to the flag: the lower the loft the more roll on the green.

• SHOT SENSE
Having played the chip, listen before looking up. Don't confuse this advice with keeping your head down.

• AFTER IMPACT
The chin is still inclined to the right and the club face is looking at, and travelling towards, the target.

LOFT •
Visualize brushing the ground on which the ball is sitting. If it lies in **rough** grass then consider a more lofted club – but remember, chips with such clubs are much harder.

• A SENSE OF TIMING
The stroke is over in just 2 seconds, but the shot remains unhurried.

SKILL

5 PITCHING

DAY 1

Definition: *Approach shot usually with wedge close to the green*

THIS LESS-THAN-FULL SHOT is best suited to shots within 55m (60yd) of the **green**. Although there are numerous ways you can pitch the ball close to the hole, the ideal pitching shot, using a pitching or **sand wedge**, should fly the ball high through the air and land it softly by the flag, followed by a minimum amount of roll.

OBJECTIVE: To clear a hazard and land on the green. *Rating* •••

─── POINTERS TO A PERFECT PITCHING SWING ───

VISUALIZATION
Visualizing the shot is necessary in every sense – so you can see the ball in your mind's eye flying high and landing in the target zone successfully. The 2 drills shown here will help you to build up a picture of how your body moves. Swinging with no arms teaches you that the upper body turns easily in the **back swing**, with a sympathetic response in the lower body. In the forward swing feel how the movement is reversed, the weight transfers, the midriff turns towards the target and the upper body responds.

SEEING THE SWING
Another useful drill to help you build up an image of the way in which your body moves and the way it should feel physically, is to practise throwing a ball underarm. The throwing arm and shoulders should feel free and relaxed. Notice that the right foot ends up on the toe with the heel pointing skywards. Unless the right foot is permitted to be released from its setting, you cannot achieve the proper forward swing. Practise both drills in front of a mirror to help you visualize. Then try with your eyes closed.

Swing with no arms

Underarm throw

Step 1
SETTING UP

Get the feel of the shot by setting up square, then move your hands counter-clockwise on the handle until the club face is open. Always align the bottom edge of the club to the hole. The more you move your hands counter-clockwise the more to the left of the target will be your body alignment. The ball position is always just left of centre in your **stance**.

• HEAD STEADY
Keep the head absolutely still throughout the shot. Always avoid hanging the head too low.

• ARMS
Let the arms swing freely down and through the ball. Never attempt to scoop the ball up or try to get the club under the ball. The wrists and hands simply follow the arm movement.

AIM •
Swing the club in the direction in which you have aligned your body – but keep the **club face** facing the hole. The bottom edge of the club is always aligned to the hole regardless of body alignment.

Pitching wedge

Loft   *Arc of swing*

DIRECTION
The line across the shoulders, hips and feet all point in the same direction – whether they are parallel with the target for less lofted shots (or shots that have more roll), or left of the target for more lofted shots (or shots with less roll).

PITCHING WEDGE
A pitching wedge is ideal for making the ball fly high, for a distance of up to 80m (90yd), and stop short, which is what you need for lofting the ball over a hazard or obstacle such as a tree or bunker.

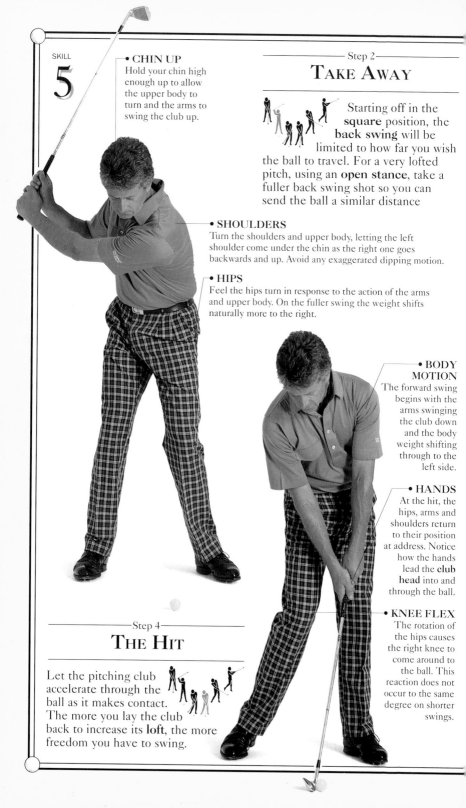

• CHIN UP
Hold your chin high
enough up to allow
the upper body to
turn and the arms to
swing the club up.

Step 2

TAKE AWAY

Starting off in the
square position, the
back swing will be
limited to how far you wish
the ball to travel. For a very lofted
pitch, using an **open stance**, take a
fuller back swing shot so you can
send the ball a similar distance

• SHOULDERS
Turn the shoulders and upper body, letting the left
shoulder come under the chin as the right one goes
backwards and up. Avoid any exaggerated dipping motion.

• HIPS
Feel the hips turn in response to the action of the arms
and upper body. On the fuller swing the weight shifts
naturally more to the right.

**• BODY
MOTION**
The forward swing
begins with the
arms swinging
the club down
and the body
weight shifting
through to the
left side.

• HANDS
At the hit, the
hips, arms and
shoulders return
to their position
at address. Notice
how the hands
lead the **club
head** into and
through the ball.

• KNEE FLEX
The rotation of
the hips causes
the right knee to
come around to
the ball. This
reaction does not
occur to the same
degree on shorter
swings.

Step 4

THE HIT

Let the pitching club
accelerate through the
ball as it makes contact.
The more you lay the club
back to increase its **loft**, the more
freedom you have to swing.

HEAD •
With the ball on its
way you can turn
your head to
follow the shot.

SHOULDERS •
After impact the
right shoulder
rotates under the
chin as the left one
goes backwards
and up.

HIPS •
The hips rotate
giving the swing
good balance and
unrestricted
movement.

KNEE •
Feel the right knee
fold naturally.

HEEL •
Right heel
comes off
the ground
as weight
is on the
left.

• HANDS
The back of the left hand faces the
sky, and so does the club face.

Step 6

FOLLOW THROUGH

 Always try to keep
your wrists from
rolling over in the
through swing: this
ensures the ball will fly high in the
direction in which the club face was
facing at the **address**. So, if you
aligned your body to the left of the
target at address, then the through
swing will also be in that direction.

• LOWER TORSO
Keep your weight firmly on left side, while
your hips and legs face the target

• FEET
Feel flexible and unrestricted in the feet.

APPROACHES TO PITCHING

ASSESSING YOUR APPROACH
• More than half the strokes most
amateurs play are usually taken from
within 75m (80yd) of the flag – so the
pitching option comes up often.
• Professionals are skilled at getting up
and down in no more than 2 shots from
within this distance from the **green**, while
most handicap golfers get to within close
proximity of the green in 2 or 3 shots, but
then take 3 or 4 more strokes to **hole out**.
This is partly because they have not
weighed up all the options and will,
regardless of the terrain or playing
conditions, attempt to trundle the ball
forwards with a 7-iron.

BACK SPIN
Many beginners fancy emulating the pros'
mastery of the back spin. However, while
you continue to play the 2-piece ball (see
p.14) designed for durability and distance
(giving more top spin and forward roll upon
landing) you are not going to get any **back
spin** when pitching on the **greens**. The
only way to get these balls to stop quickly
on the greens is to hit them higher, laying
the club back to increase the **loft**.

WHEN IT PAYS TO PITCH
When the ball is not lying well or there are
obstacles to clear, then be prepared to play
the pitching option.

SKILL

5

PITCHING IN ACTION

Familiarize yourself with certain
consistencies in the pitching swing.
Notice that the head remains still until
the conclusion of the shot, while the hips
rotate towards the target. The shoulders
and arms maintain a constant triangle
throughout the action.

• BODY WEIGHT
Body weight is planted firmly on the left
hand side before, during, and after impact.
As the upper body turns, the lower body
follows naturally in order to
accommodate the swing action.

BACK SWING •
There is a definite lagging of
the **club head** in the initial
stages. The wrists are
cocked at the apex of
the **back swing**.

STANCE •
The right heel lifts slightly
in mid swing, allowing the
hips and midriff to turn
towards the target.

SWING THOUGHTS

SWING NOT SCOOP

Never attempt to scoop the club under the ball in an attempt to gain extra lift. Concentrate on a fluid swing and an accurate aim; allow the loft of the club face to take care of the rest as it passes through the ball. Remember to allow your right heel to rise slightly as you swing easily through the ball; failure to do this will almost certainly result in a mishit.

PREPARATION

When practising, place a tee peg in the ground about 10-12cm (4-5in) from the ball on the target side. Play the shot, taking both the ball and the tee peg. This encourages you to take an extended forward swing with the club head low to the ground through impact. Alternatively, visualize brushing the club head along the grass before playing the shot.

• EYES DOWN

Resist the temptation to look up too early. Stay down on the shot and keep your eyes on the spot where the ball was placed.

BALANCE •

Balance is maintained as the hips and legs turn towards the target. The back of the left hand faces the sky, resisting the urge to roll over.

FOLLOW THROUGH •

Notice that the swing does not follow through fully. Rather like a lob in tennis, the emphasis is on lift and accuracy. The swing should be easy and relaxed ... almost lazy in feel.

FULL SWING

Definition: *A series of natural body reactions,
not a sequence of contortions*

DAY 1

THE GOLF SWING consists of two turns of the
body with one swing of the arms around a central
axis point. The **club head** travels in an arc and its
speed at impact, as well as the rhythm, tempo and
timing of the movements of the arms and body,
are controlled from the revolving centre. Study the player
here, taking in the general picture of the stroke.

OBJECTIVE: To apply the **club face** correctly at impact,
at speed, to give you control of the ball. *Rating* •••••

UPPER BODY•
Poise yourself and
feel relaxed and
ready for action.
Don't put your
head down and
don't leave the
left arm rigidly
straight: these two
misconceptions
ruin good play.

SUPPORT •
Keep your pelvic
area down and to
the back, and flex
your knees to give
the arms and hands
space to hang
freely below the
chin. Feel the
hips and knees
bearing the
weight of the
body.

————— Step 1 —————
ADDRESS

Align the **club face** to
the target, and the body
parallel to the **target
line** with a posture that
will swing the club on a **swing plane**
best suited to the design of your club

PASSIVE PLAY
Keep everything
above the line of the
club **shaft** – the
muscles of the hands,
arms, stomach,
shoulders, back and
face – passive.
Everything below the
line – legs, knees and
feet – must be springy.

•CLUB FACE
Swing the **club face** so that it looks down
the **target line** – the ball will travel there.

HEAD •
Keep the chin up and incline it a little to the right. Rotate the head slightly, but don't let it sway.

HALF SWING •
Acquaint yourself with the half swing at first. Take the club back to waist high. The club points directly away from the target with its toe pointing upwards to the sky. The right elbow begins to fold but the left arm remains comfortably extended. The weight of the body is beginning to transfer over to the right foot as the hips and legs react.

Step 2
EARLY TAKE AWAY

The early take away and full back swing form a smooth, one-piece action where the arms swing the club away from the ball (the club head low to the ground in the early stage) and the upper body turns out of the way comfortably.

• KNEES
Let the left knee come round to the ball, but do not move the right knee at all.

• GRIP
Maintain a constant light hold on the handle all through the movement. Don't hinge the wrists until the end.

• HIPS
Feel the hips respond to the full turn of the shoulders and upper body.

Step 3
BACK SWING

Don't deliberate over the **back swing** movement. Liken it to the loading of a spring – the upper body turns as the arms swing up and the lower body responds. Maintain the posture of the spine as it rotates on its constant **angle of tilt**.

• LEGS
Avoid tension and rigidity in the legs

WEIGHT TRANSFER •
As the upper body rotates, feel the automatic follow-on response from the hips and legs as the weight transfers to the right.

SKILL

6

HEAD •
Keep your head still with the chin inclined to the right.

ARMS •
The arms and hands lead the **club head**. They are free-falling and are being pulled around by the hip rotation as well as by the weight transfer.

BALANCE •
Avoid any action with your golf swing that might lead to over-balancing.

WEIGHT •
Make sure the weight transfers to the left foot long before the club arrives at the ball.

Step 4

FORWARD SWING

The spring, once set, is released by the following order of movement: the lower body rotates, transferring its weight to the front foot, then come the arms and, lastly, the **club head**.

SWING PATH
In the **back swing** the club tracks away from the ball on an arc inside the **target line**, and up. At the start of the forward swing, the club returns down on the same **swing path** as though moving outwards and away from you.

• EYES
Look at the ball long enough to see the contact; then follow it.

Step 5

THROUGH SWING

In the **through swing** the transfer of weight and unwinding of the hips become the power source of the shot. To apply the **club face** so it faces the target on impact, keep a steady purchase on the grip, allowing no feeling of release with the hands.

HIPS •
Allow the hips to clear and so make room for the arms as they swing through the ball.

CONTROL
Don't "swish" the club head too early or you'll lose force.

• HAN[I]
Keep the grip stead[y] throughou[t] the swing[.]

SHOULDERS •
During the forward and
through swing the right
shoulder comes down
and under the chin as
the left shoulder goes
backwards and up.
This maintains the
same **angle of tilt** of
the spine as set up at
the address.

HIPS •
The hips revolve like an
unwinding spring around
the centre of your body.

FEET •
To ensure a full and
free turn through to
the target, allow the
right heel to come
out of the ground.
Let the feet take
part in the full
swing to keep a
perfectly balanced
flowing action.

— Step 6 —
FOLLOW THROUGH

Feel the full **follow
through** as a natural
reaction to every-
thing that has gone
before. The club swings all the way
up and around the left ear as your
hips unwind, and you maintain
perfect balance because your full
swing is revolving around the
centre of your body.

FEEL THE SWING
See the swing as a whole
– not as a series of
physical actions. Look at
the ball, but feel and be
aware of the rhythm and
ease of the movement.
You cannot play good golf
by thinking about the
ball. Try some practice
swings to get accustomed
to the feel of the swing
movement. Then make
sure your golf shot has
the same feel.

SWING SENSATION

DON'T FORCE IT
The **club head** speed at impact and, as a
result, the distance you can drive the
ball, comes from the free-flowing
elasticity of your swing – and not from
applied force.

PICTURE THIS
Picture the **path** of the **back swing**, and
observe the club head coming back on
the same path.

RHYTHM
Make sure the forward swing begins at
the same easy **pace** as the **back swing**
begins. Experiment with your **tempo** to
find out which speed suits you best.

DRIVING
Swinging with a **wood** is just as with an
iron – but you will need a **tee peg** for
teeing off to ensure a good **trajectory**.

SKILL

6

• **FULL TURN**
Turn fully allowing your
back to face the target
and the club will be
aimed at the target in
readiness for the
next reaction.

FULL SWING IN ACTION

Study this sequence several times in
swift succession – without stopping to
isolate any single position – and
capture the flow of the movement.
The upper body turns as the arms
swing up, then the arms are swung
down as the hips unwind. It is this
effortless interaction that produces
club head speed and distance in a
state of balance.

DOWN SWING •
The transfer of weight
from the back foot to
the front at the
beginning of the
forward movement
brings the arms
downwards.

IMPACT •
At this point feel the club move outwards and
away from you. Don't force the action – arm
movements respond naturally to body
movement – the hands and arms simply do
nothing but respond.

SWING SENSATION

BALANCE
Never allow your golf swing to interfere with your balance. You can only establish true balance when that part of the body nearest the ground – the lower torso – begins to dominate the swing action.

SPEED
Fast or slow is fine – as long as the swing is rhythmical.

TIMING
The arms and the body should move independently of, but synchronized with, each other.

RHYTHM
See the movement backwards and forwards as being superimposed.

TEMPO
Experiment with your **tempo** to get the most effective swing.

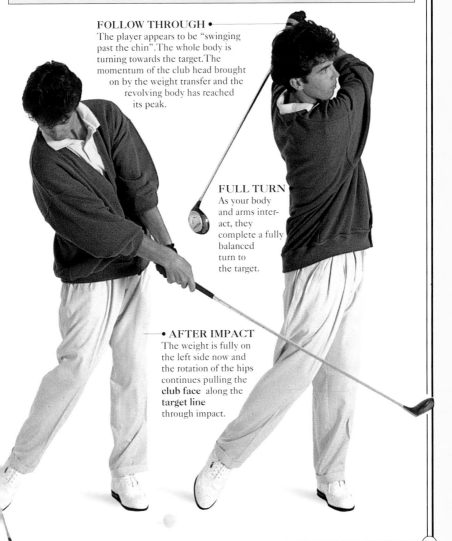

FOLLOW THROUGH •
The player appears to be "swinging past the chin". The whole body is turning towards the target. The momentum of the club head brought on by the weight transfer and the revolving body has reached its peak.

FULL TURN
As your body and arms interact, they complete a fully balanced turn to the target.

• **AFTER IMPACT**
The weight is fully on the left side now and the rotation of the hips continues pulling the **club face** along the **target line** through impact.

SKILL

DAY 2

7 BALL CONTROL

Definition: *Placing and playing accurate shots when **club face** alignment is not square to its **swing path** or target*

CLUB FACE ALIGNMENT MUST BE square to its **swing path** if the ball is to fly directly to its target. However, you may not always want the ball to fly directly, because a tree or another obstacle is in the way. It may seem amazing how professionals, unable to see the green, can bend the ball around that tree in their path and land it safely on the target – yet the principles can be easily understood by the inexperienced player. Understanding ball control will enable you to consider the option of playing indirectly, and ultimately, with the necessary practice, to play **hooks** and **slices** intentionally.

OBJECTIVE: To send the ball directly or indirectly to your initial target.
Rating •••••

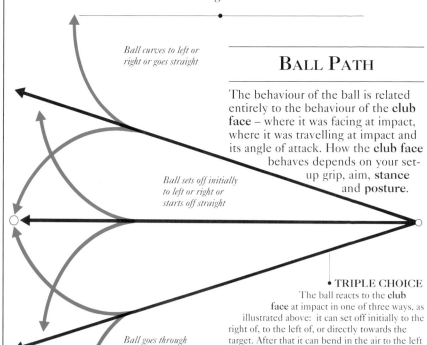

Ball curves to left or right or goes straight

BALL PATH

The behaviour of the ball is related entirely to the behaviour of the **club face** – where it was facing at impact, where it was travelling at impact and its angle of attack. How the **club face** behaves depends on your set-up grip, aim, **stance** and **posture**.

Ball sets off initially to left or right or starts off straight

• **TRIPLE CHOICE**
The ball reacts to the **club face** at impact in one of three ways, as illustrated above: it can set off initially to the right of, to the left of, or directly towards the target. After that it can bend in the air to the left of, to the right of, or fly directly on in its initial direction of flight. The ball can also fly through the air or roll along the ground.

Ball goes through air or on ground

• **EYES**
Watch the part of
the ball with which
the club face
makes contact.

• **SHOULDERS**
Notice the right
shoulder is set
slightly lower than
the left. The line
across the torso
and hips is parallel
to the **target line**.

• **HANDS**
Your arms and
hands hang loosely
downwards, with
the hips well out of
the way as the
pelvic area is set
backwards and
down.

INITIAL DIRECTION

Body **alignment** in the **address**
position influences the direction in
which the ball sets off. The body
rotates to the right in the **back swing**
and to the left in the **through swing**.

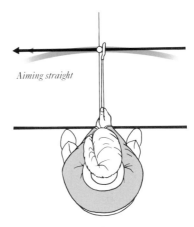

Aiming straight

SQUARE STANCE
To stand square to the target means having
the **club face** face the hole with the body
aligned at right angles to its leading edge. It
is a feeling of being sideways-on to the hole.

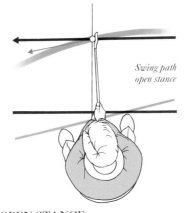

*Swing path
closed stance*

*Swing path
open stance*

CLOSED STANCE
A stance is **closed** when the lines across
the shoulders, hips and toes are aimed to
the right of the target regardless of
the direction in which the club face is facing.

OPEN STANCE
A stance is open when the lines across the
shoulders, hips and toes are aimed to the left
of target. Practise laying a club on the floor
and stand open, square and closed to it.

SKILL

7

STRAIGHT SHOT

For the straight shot aim to present the **club face** square to the target at impact. Regardless of the club's loft the ball will simply fly forwards.

CLUB FACE ALIGNMENT

Having grasped the first principle of body alignment which influences the initial direction of the shot, you must now understand how **club face** alignment at impact puts spin on the ball to make it bend in the air. The hands control the club face depending on how you place them on the handle, and this influences the direction in which the club face will look at impact.

• GRIP FEEL

Whatever the hands do the **club face** will do likewise. Hold the club by its handle out in front of you with the grip as illustrated. The toe of the club points to the sky with the **grooves** going north-to-south. When you rotate the hands to the right the club face moves accordingly – it also moves as the hands rotate to the left.

• NEUTRAL POSITION

When the hands are in this neutral position the "V"s formed by the thumb and forefingers point somewhere between your right ear and shoulder. This hand to handle arrangement returns the **club face** square, so any adjustment of the grip causes the club face to react in another fashion.

THE CLUB FACE GAME

WHERE, NOT HOW

• Getting the gist of how to swing the club correctly is naturally a key skill to achieve, but not by copying body movements and techniques – as the body does not hit the golf ball. It is the club face that hits the ball, so ball control through **club face** alignment, not through the swing of the club, is what you need to learn.

• In your eagerness to hit the ball well avoid trying to attain a swing style and instead practise how to present the club face to the ball. As golf is a game where the ball is stationary until the moment of contact, be careful not to over-analyze ball control because this could lead you to seize up.

• Avoid thinking about how to swing the club but picture and plan where you wish to send the ball.

SHAPE YOUR SHOTS

Many of the world's leading players came up through the caddy ranks. Having little or no money they carried the professionals' bags and observed the game being played at close quarters. They quickly understood how to make the ball fly high or low and how to make it bend to the left or right. Having watched the swings of their employers they quickly learnt that there was no substitute for rhythm, tempo and balance. Above all they learnt that golf was a **club face** game, and that the manner in which they held the club and stood around the club and ball – rather than how they swung the club – enabled them to achieve control of the ball.

• Practise holding your club as illustrated and learn from the natural reaction of the ball. Visualize shaping the shot.

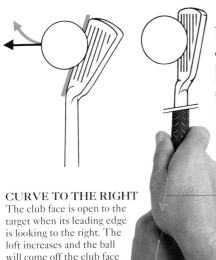

OPENED CLUB FACE

Ball control enables you either to correct a fault or to build in a specific reaction such as making the ball fly higher, or moving it left to right in the air deliberately. To achieve this use a longer club such as a 4- or 5-iron. Have fun with this, remembering that by exaggerating things at this early stage you will learn more quickly.

CURVE TO THE RIGHT
The club face is open to the target when its leading edge is looking to the right. The loft increases and the ball will come off the club face with a clockwise spin. This makes the ball fly higher than normal and curve to the right.

• WEAKENED GRIP
Take your club in your hands with the club face as illustrated. Weaken your grip by making the "V"s of both hands move and point to the left of your chin. As you hold the club lightly in this fashion rotate the hands back to the right into their natural hitting position and observe how the **club face** opens.

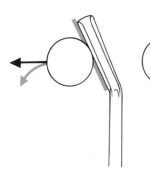

CLOSED CLUB FACE

Whichever golf skill you are trying to learn, remember that to have control of the ball is to have control of the **club face**. To have control of the club face is to know that the position of the hands on the handle at the outset sets up the reactions which follow.

CURVE TO THE LEFT
Having a closed **club face** at impact will cause the ball to **spin** in a counter-clockwise fashion. The ball will fly lower than usual and travel further as the **club face** impacts on the ball with hardly any **loft**, sending the ball to the left.

• STRENGTHENED GRIP
With the club face square, as illustrated, hold the club lightly with the "V"s of both hands pointing well over to your right shoulder. You will see all 4 knuckles of the left hand. Rotate your hands back to their neutral position where you can see the first 2 knuckles of each hand and the **club face** closes. Take your 4- or 5-iron and play some shots. Don't worry about a specific target.

SKILL

7 SWING PLANE

Body alignment at address and club face alignment at impact are the first two principles of ball control. The swing plane is the third, and is largely dictated by the length of the club you use. Imagine using a club 15m (50ft) long. This would demand a more exaggerated horizontal swing plane than a club which was only ½m (2ft) long. Picture this clearly in your mind's eye.

SHALLOW FORWARD SWING

Longer clubs, such as the driver shown here, determine a shallower swing plane. Also the forward swing tends to be slightly flatter than the back swing.

STEEP BACKWARD SWING

Shorter clubs, as with the more lofted irons, determine a steeper swing plane or angle of attack. Moreover, the plane of the back swing is generally steeper than that of the forward swing.

• BACK SWING POSTURE

The upper body turns as the arms swing the club up, but the club will be swung out of the plane if the posture of the spine changes. Poor shots result when, in the back swing, the left shoulder either dips down towards the ball (causing too steep a plane) or when it rises too high (causing a flat plane). The upper body rotates on a constant angle of tilt as the arms swing up.

• BACK SWING PLANE

The arms swing the club higher than the upper body turns in the backward swing, and the plane of the back swing on straight shots is steeper than that of the forward swing.

START BACK

Mistakes are usually built-in at the **address**, but most errors occur in the first metre (3ft) of the back swing. Avoid any independent hand, wrist or forearm action in the initial stages of the **take away**. Start back square, allowing the upper body, arms, hands, and **club face** to turn away from the ball in a smooth one-piece action.

CLUB LOW •
Aim to keep the club face low to the ground as you start the **take away**, and your upper body turns.

BODY TURN •
When your mid-section has turned about 30° swing your arms up – but keep turning.

HANDS •
Allow the wrists to hinge comfortably – but not until your upper body has all but completed its wind-up. When you feel the left thumb to be under the handle the club face will be in its correct hitting position.

SPINNING THOUGHTS

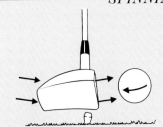

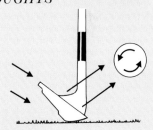

SIDE SPIN
Understanding body **alignment**, **club-face** alignment and **swing plane** shows you that long clubs (with less **loft** which means they move naturally on a flatter swing plane) produce side spin on the ball. This in turn causes the ball to bend in the air in the direction in which the club face was facing at impact.

BACK SPIN
Shorter, more lofted, clubs like a pitching wedge, induce a much steeper angle of attack which in turn imparts **back spin**. This causes the ball to fly true, without curving in the air, in a direction in which the club face was looking at impact. Practise with a wood or long iron (off a **tee peg** at first) and a pitching wedge – to learn ball reactions.

SKILL

7

BENDING THE BALL RIGHT

Apply the fundamentals learnt on pp.56-61 to bend the ball around an obstacle such as a tree. Imagine what you want the ball to do, then adopt a set up and grip that gives you the desired ball reaction.

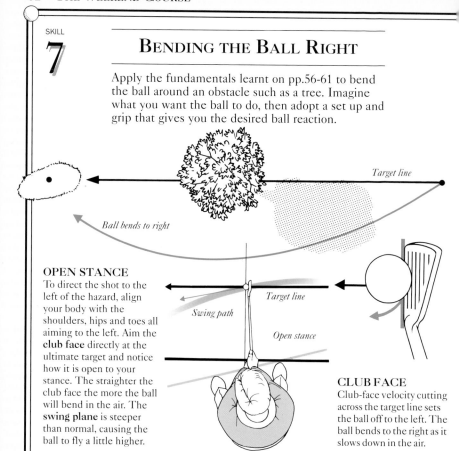

Target line

Ball bends to right

Target line

Swing path

Open stance

OPEN STANCE
To direct the shot to the left of the hazard, align your body with the shoulders, hips and toes all aiming to the left. Aim the **club face** directly at the ultimate target and notice how it is open to your stance. The straighter the club face the more the ball will bend in the air. The **swing plane** is steeper than normal, causing the ball to fly a little higher.

CLUB FACE
Club-face velocity cutting across the target line sets the ball off to the left. The ball bends to the right as it slows down in the air.

— TROUBLE SHOOTING —

CURING COMMON FAULTS
Golfers frequently think that they are doing everything properly with each hit but become frustrated by their inconsistent results. One good shot seems to be followed by several poor ones. So what can you do about this?
• Let the ball be your ultimate instructor. The way it reacts tells you exactly how the club was aligned and in which direction it was moving at the moment of impact. Then you can try to cure the fault.

ACCEPT MISTAKES
Golf is a game of mistakes: a game of "nearlies", "almosts" and "not quites". Nothing is a problem until a pattern of shots emerges which is potentially destructive to overall performance.

CURING HOOKS AND SLICES
• Shots that curve to the right mean that at impact the **club face** was open to its **swing path** producing clockwise spin on the ball. Study the illustration on p.59 and adopt a strong grip. If the ball bends unintentionally to the left, move both hands to the left in a weaker grip. Also make sure that your posture is correct. Standing too close to, or too far away from, the ball will affect the **swing path** of your club.
• Shots setting off to the left of the target mean the club is travelling to the right. Perhaps your hips and toes are aligned properly, but your shoulders are open and aiming left; or your whole body alignment is aiming left, or your ball position is too far forward in the stance.

BENDING THE BALL LEFT

The ball which travels from right to left flies lower and rolls further upon landing, so you may need to use a less powerful club for this shot. Don't consciously alter your swing and hold the club lightly.

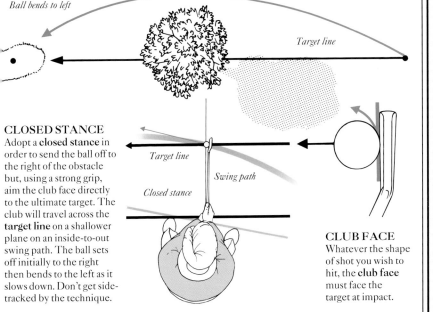

Ball bends to left

Target line

Target line

Swing path

Closed stance

CLOSED STANCE

Adopt a **closed stance** in order to send the ball off to the right of the obstacle but, using a strong grip, aim the club face directly to the ultimate target. The club will travel across the **target line** on a shallower plane on an inside-to-out swing path. The ball sets off initially to the right then bends to the left as it slows down. Don't get side-tracked by the technique.

CLUB FACE

Whatever the shape of shot you wish to hit, the **club face** must face the target at impact.

TROUBLE SHOOTING

• Shots setting off to the right of the target, meaning the club is moving right of target, could be the result of your **alignment** being too much to the right, or the ball being too far back in the stance.

OUT OF CONTROL

Here is what goes wrong when the ball shoots off out of control:

• Ball sets off left – the shoulders heave the club down and across the target line (usually as a result of trying to hit the ball hard); or an early casting of the club head from the top of the back swing causes the weight to remain on the back foot as the club is pulled around to face left of the target at impact.

• Ball sets off to the right – the arms swing down faster than the lower body can clear out of the way (hitting the ground in front of the ball is a clue); or the hips slide laterally in the forward swing without rotating; or there is insufficient turn of the upper body (particularly on longer clubs), which leaves the club face open – never having given it a chance to square up by impact.

• Problems are not so difficult to solve if you first understand what you are setting up, and secondly if you come to grips with the timing of the swing.

G.A.S.P.

Remember, your club responds to the 4 key setting-up phases: **G**rip, **A**im, **S**tance, Posture (G.A.S.P. for short). Grasp the basics of G.A.S.P. to understand club and ball behaviour.

SKILL

8 BUNKER PLAY

DAY 2

Definition: *A shot played from sand. Fairway bunkers are generally shallower than those by the greens*

ALTHOUGH BUNKERS ARE AS MUCH a psychological as a physical obstacle to confident golf, bunker shots are in danger of being over-analyzed. Just learn a few basic ground rules and don't analyze it any further.

OBJECTIVE: Getting the ball out first time. *Rating* •••

--- Step 1 ---

ADDRESS

Bunker shots require a change in **address**, but the swing remains the same. Swing the club so that it enters the sand a few centimetres before the ball and leaves the sand a few centimetres after it. Hit the sand, not the ball.

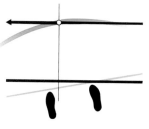

ALIGNMENT
Aim the **club face** to the target but align your shoulders, hips and feet 1–2m (3–6ft) to the left.

• **EYES**
Focus the eyes a few centimetres behind the ball – that should be your point of entry – not on the ball itself.

• **HANDS IN LINE**
As you look down, your hands are to the left of the **club head**, forming a straight line from the club head to the left shoulder.

• **BALL**
The ball is positioned between the centre of your **stance** and left heel. Remember, you are not allowed to touch the ball, or sand, in the **address** position.

SWINGING THROUGH THE SAND

SAND WEDGE
For a straightforward shot use the **sand wedge**. The proud shoulder on its **sole** glides the club smoothly through the sand.

VISUALIZE YOUR SWING
Getting the gist of it is the key. Even though your upper body rotates, it maintains its posture and balance on a constant axis. Your left shoulder comes down and under your chin, while your right shoulder goes backwards and up, taking your arms up to the full swing. Your hips respond in sympathy and weight transfers from your left to your right.

Step 2

TAKE AWAY

After aligning yourself to the left of the target, swing in that direction. The **club face** facing the hole will cause the ball to pop up, fly towards the hole and land gently.

• **SWING**
Swinging in the sand does not differ from the normal golf swing – but the set up does. You need a steeper **swing plane** to get under the sand and below the ball.

• **AIM**
Aim to take the ball out on a cushion of sand – don't go for the ball itself.

FEET •
Secure a firm foothold by wriggling your feet in the sand – the left foot a little deeper than the right.

• **KNEES**
The left knee comes around to the ball, while the right retains its flex comfortably.

TOP OF THE SWING
The spine rotates on a constant **angle of tilt**. The arms are fully swung up but there has been no lifting of the body. The club points in the same direction as the feet alignment.

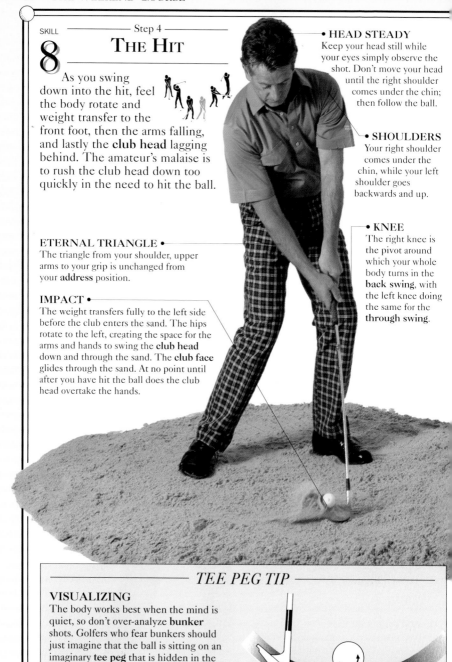

SKILL

8

— Step 4 —
THE HIT

As you swing down into the hit, feel the body rotate and weight transfer to the front foot, then the arms falling, and lastly the **club head** lagging behind. The amateur's malaise is to rush the club head down too quickly in the need to hit the ball.

• HEAD STEADY
Keep your head still while your eyes simply observe the shot. Don't move your head until the right shoulder comes under the chin; then follow the ball.

• SHOULDERS
Your right shoulder comes under the chin, while your left shoulder goes backwards and up.

• KNEE
The right knee is the pivot around which your whole body turns in the **back swing**, with the left knee doing the same for the **through swing**.

ETERNAL TRIANGLE •
The triangle from your shoulder, upper arms to your grip is unchanged from your **address** position.

IMPACT •
The weight transfers fully to the left side before the club enters the sand. The hips rotate to the left, creating the space for the arms and hands to swing the **club head** down and through the sand. The **club face** glides through the sand. At no point until after you have hit the ball does the club head overtake the hands.

TEE PEG TIP

VISUALIZING
The body works best when the mind is quiet, so don't over-analyze **bunker** shots. Golfers who fear bunkers should just imagine that the ball is sitting on an imaginary **tee peg** that is hidden in the sand. Visualize your swing as if you're hitting the tee peg on to the **green**, right up there by the hole, and forget the ball. Let the club face glide through the sand.

Tee peg

Step 5
FOLLOW THROUGH

The **club face** and ball never meet in a good **bunker** shot. The club face takes the sand, which takes the ball. Swing fully through the sand.

• ARMS
The more **loft** the higher the ball flies, so allow your arms to swing freely with the **club face** lagging behind and still facing the target.

FULL SWING
As there is no bounce off the sand you must play a full swing right through.

CLUB •
The club follows the path of your alignment at **address**: so long as the **club face** faces the target, the ball will fly to the target.

BURIED IN THE BUNKER

TEXTURE
The sand's texture will make a difference to your swing: if it is light and powdery the club will glide through easily. In coarse and wet sand you'll need a more powerful swinging action. Place your feet well into the sand to secure a firm footing, but keep them lively. Your left heel will naturally come a little off the ground in the back swing to aid your balance.

PLUGGED IN
If the ball is truly buried, aim the **club face** to the left of the target and align yourself to the right of the target, positioning the ball nearer your right foot. Cock your wrist early so that the club picks up steeply and release the wrists early in the down swing aiming to hit the top of the ball. Not an elegant shot, but it works well for balls plugged into the sand.

SKILL

8

BUNKER SHOT IN ACTION

With this "splash" shot, you can sense the ease, rhythm, and fullness of swing. The player opens his club face, opens his stance, and follows normally to the end of the follow through. There is no need to use applied force.

• **ALIGNMENT**
The body is aligned to the left creating a steeper angle of descent for the swing.

• **BACK SWING**
The upper body turns to initiate the **back swing** while the lower body transfers the weight and rotates towards the target to accommodate the forward swing.

SWING THOUGHTS

FIRM FOOTING
Ignore the ball; it is a cushion of sand behind and under it that you wish to put on to the green. Always twist your feet into the sand to secure a good platform for the swing. In damp, firmly packed sand, try using a pitching wedge in place of the **sand wedge**.

SWING STYLE
Some players vary the amount of swing to make the ball fly a greater or lesser distance. Others take a full swing, but vary the amount of sand they take with the shot. The less sand, the greater the distance. Try both methods to see which of them suits you best.

FOLLOW THROUGH •
Allow the arms to respond to the turning of the body for a full, effortless **follow through**.

• FULL SWING
The swing is expanded creating a fullness of arc with the club face still looking at the target.

SKILL 9 PLAYING AWKWARD LIES

DAY 2

Definition: *When the ground gets in the way of the swing*

BETWEEN THE **TEEING GROUND** and the putting **green** lies much hazardous territory, with sloping terrain and uneven contours. Chances are you will be forced to play from awkward positions – be it uphill, downhill or along a slope – because of the course layout. Whatever the lie, remember to swing the club through the ball; make good contact on the ball; and feel balanced during the swing.

OBJECTIVE: Good recovery shots from rough, uneven terrain. *Rating* •••••

UPHILL STANCE

Adopt a set up that encourages a good **through swing**, contact and balance. If you have these 3 factors right, then the swing will fall into place naturally. Do not panic because it seems hard.

ARMS •
Align the shoulders to sit parallel to the slope so that you can swing the club through the ball. The shoulders must be totally relaxed. Feel your swing action coming mainly from the arms, because 2 full turns of the body becomes difficult to achieve from this position.

• HIPS
Keep your hips and waistline parallel with the ground, easing the swing up the slope.

• HIGHER FOOT
Position the ball nearer the higher foot for hitting uphill and aim a little to the right of your target to compensate for the ball naturally tending to fly to the left. Let it.

BALANCE •
Notice how the shoulder alignment causes the body weight to settle on to the lower foot. Focus on keeping balanced.

ANGLE OF ATTACK

Don't try to achieve a full **back swing** in this uncomfortable and sometimes precarious position, because you are in danger of losing your balance. Stay relaxed in the shoulders and let the arms swing freely. Allow your **swing plane** to be naturally shallow or flat.

• CLEAN SWEEP
Swing the club around rather than up with your arms. Aim to sweep the ball up the slope.

THROUGH SWING
The **through swing** is much fuller than the **back swing**. The arms swing all the way through the ball. Loss of balance in the uphill swing is likely; if so, let it happen.

• SHOULDER
Keep the shoulders, as well as the back, totally passive.

• LEGS
There is very little leg action at any stage during the swing. The lie of the land makes it difficult for the legs to do anything to assist in the movement – they are too busy trying to hold your balance.

6-iron

6-iron

CLUB CHOICE
The slope causes the club to increase in **loft** as you address the ball uphill. So a 6-iron effectively does the work of an 8-iron on an elevated slope (above). The ball will naturally fly to the left.

SKILL

9 DOWNHILL STANCE

Use the same techniques for playing downhill as for uphill play, even though your stance is quite different. Downward slopes make restrictions on your set up, balance, support and all body movements. Both uphill and downhill play requires a sweeping shot where you swing with the slope. Do not try to pick the ball off the surface with the wrists – it's too risky.

• BALANCE
Depending upon the severity of the slope, balance the body weight well forward with the shoulders angled to suit the contour of the slope and the head almost over the lower foot.

• SUPPORT
Let the hips and knees take the strain as they work hard to maintain steadiness in preparation for and during the action.

• CLUB CHOICE
Use a more lofted (less powerful) club for the distance required.

HANG LOOSE •
Let your arms hang loose ready to perform nearly all of the work.

• BALL
Position yourself with the ball once again near the higher foot, only this time the higher foot is the back one.

KEEPING DOWNWARDLY MOBILE

DOWNHILL SWING
The ball flies lower and further from a downhill lie, so use a more lofted (less powerful) club than for a flat-lie shot of the same distance. The ball sits near the higher foot which makes it set off to the right. It will go even further right as the **club face** is open because of the steep **swing plane** (angle of attack) – so aim left.

DOWNHILL PITCH
Adopt an open stance with a pitching or **sand wedge**. Keep steady on the lower foot, knees flexed, wrists firm and club face open. Sweep down the slope.

DOWNHILL BUNKER
On the downhill slope of a bunker, play the ball further back in the **stance**. Align the shoulders to the slope and lay the club face open. The **back swing** is a steep lift of the arms. Aim to hit behind the ball and follow through down the slope. The ball will come out from the downhill stance lower, and will roll further.

DOWNHILL CHIP
On long downhill chip shots use an 8- or a 9-iron adopting a regular stance but with the ball just a little bit back of centre. Keep the **club face** square, or facing to the target.

ANGLE OF ATTACK

The steeper the slope, the more awkward the stroke feels as all your body weight goes on the lower foot. Although the upper body does rotate, the **back swing** is made with the arms lifting the club up steeply, while the hips and legs remain still as they struggle to keep their balance.

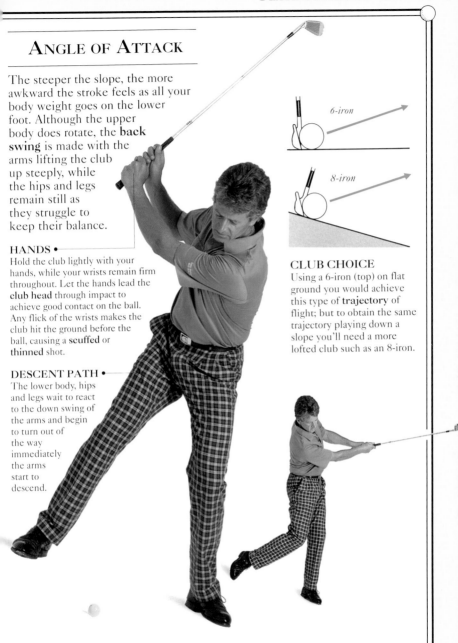

HANDS •
Hold the club lightly with your hands, while your wrists remain firm throughout. Let the hands lead the **club head** through impact to achieve good contact on the ball. Any flick of the wrists makes the club hit the ground before the ball, causing a **scuffed** or **thinned** shot.

DESCENT PATH •
The lower body, hips and legs wait to react to the down swing of the arms and begin to turn out of the way immediately the arms start to descend.

6-iron

8-iron

CLUB CHOICE
Using a 6-iron (top) on flat ground you would achieve this type of **trajectory** of flight; but to obtain the same trajectory playing down a slope you'll need a more lofted club such as an 8-iron.

PLAY SHORT
The ball flies lower and rolls more on the downhill shots (the opposite is true when playing awkward uphill shots). Play your shots to land short of the green allowing for the lower **trajectory** and greater roll of the ball.

FOLLOW THROUGH
Swing the club down the slope with your arms, as your body rotates towards the target. Feel the release from the discomfort of the stance after impact and be ready to lose balance.

SKILL
9

AIM
If the slope is only slight there is no need to aim to the right.

SHOULDERS
Keep the shoulders relaxed and aligned to the hips, **stance** and **target line**.

POSTURE
Keep the spine comfortably straight and leaning rather less from the hips.

A FIRM BASE
Flex the knees slightly and hold the legs steady to create a firm base for the swing.

SLOPING STANCE
With your body weight more on the toes than on the heels, you'll get the impression of leaning towards the slope.

BALL ABOVE STANCE

Playing across the slope requires further stance and set up adjustments. Body **alignment** and balance are again the crucial factors, as is a good contact with the ball. Standing with the ball above the level of the feet effectively brings you closer to the ball, so stand more upright.

GRIP
Shorten the grip by holding the club further down the handle.

CLUB CHOICE
Use the club for the distance required, as if playing from a flat lie.

BALL ADDRESS
With longer, less lofted clubs, position yourself with the ball in the centre of the **stance**. Bring the ball even nearer the right foot when using shorter, more lofted irons because they cause the ball to pull more to the left.

A SIDEHILL STRUGGLE

FLIGHT PATH
Whether you are facing or backing on to the slope, the ball will always bend in the air in the direction of the down slope.

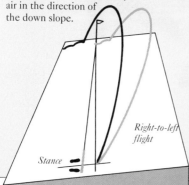

Right-to-left flight

Stance

UNCOMFORTABLE TRUTHS
• Standing below the ball forces you into a more upright stance, a shortened grip, and balancing towards the toes. All this is necessary to ensure solid contact with the ball.
• To guarantee a good hit you should normally play the ball in the centre of your stance, but with severe lies your lower half cannot swing with the upper half because it is trying to prevent you falling over, and also your arms cannot clear out of the way. So it is therefore best to play the ball from a position right of centre, as this allows for the bend to the left in flight as well as allowing for the greater roll to the left when the ball hits the green.

TAKE AWAY •
The arms lead
the **club face**
independently
of the
lower body.

ANGLE OF ATTACK

As you take back the club, swing the club away
from the ball with your arms and feel the
shoulders and upper body turn in sympathy.
However, hips and legs are restricted by their
effort to keep balance on the slope.

SHOULDERS •
The shoulders
rotate on an
extremely flat
swing plane in
such an awkward
lie, but this is
consistent with
having to stand
tall to the ball.

HIP •
The hips also rotate
on a flat **swing plane,**
although too much
movement will cause
loss of balance
depending on the
severity of the slope.

FOLLOW THROUGH
Balance is the key throughout the
above **stance** swing, especially in
the follow through. Let the arms
swing the club independently of
the body to help your balance.

LOWER BODY •
Leg action is minimal
for this shot – quite
unlike the full swing on
a flat surface where the
hips, legs and feet play a
major role in an efficient,
sound swing.

MIND OVER BODY
Think about making a good, clean contact.
Remember that golf is a game of feel and, as
with all awkward shots, your performance
will be reflected by how you perceive it. Tell
yourself that it is easy and it will be. But if
you see it as difficult, then you will certainly
find it impossible to succeed.

QUESTION OF BALANCE
In the ball above stance position, the hips
cannot swing round fully, the posture
remains upright and the **swing plane** (or
angle of attack) stays flatter throughout the
swing than it would with a normal lie shot.
To help you maintain good balance try to
keep your shoulders free of tension.

BALL BELOW STANCE

Your **stance** is dictated by the sloping away terrain and by your need to maintain balance and establish clean contact. The only way to play this uncomfortable shot well is by ensuring that your muscles feel relaxed – and you feel balanced.

• CONCENTRATE
You cannot achieve great power and distance with sidehill shots, and you can only achieve successful results if you concentrate on keeping your balance.

• ARM ALIGNMENT
Allow the arms to hang straight down and, assuming that the ball is not in long grass, hold the club lightly.

POSTURE •
Lean back into the hill and keep the spine straight. If you bend over from the waist now, you will probably topple over.

• GRIP
The ball sits further away from you, being below the level of your stance, so you need to lengthen your grip and bring the butt of the handle on to the palm of the left hand.

LOWER BODY SUPPORT •
There is quite a lot of strain on the back of the legs, but notice how the buttocks serve as a counterbalance to the head, and how the body sits over the knees and feet.

• CENTRE STANCE
Try to play the ball off the centre stance for all clubs, to ensure clean contact.

FEET •
Support your weight firmly back on the heels.

• ON TARGET
If the slope is severe, just hit the ball in the general direction of the target.

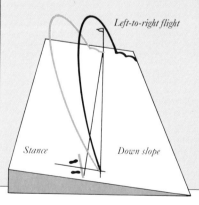

SLOPE AND SWING

Left-to-right flight

Stance   *Down slope*

STEEP SWING
Standing above the ball restricts your **back swing** to a very steep **swing plane** (angle of attack). The further the distance you have to hit the ball, the more impossible it becomes to present the **club face square** to the target at impact. Because of the steepness of your swing plane, your club face will be facing to the right at impact and this will send the ball off further to the right. So aim to the left to compensate for this. It is your **club face** alignment in relation to its **swing plane** that influences the spin on the ball and its direction.

RESTRICTED SWING •
Both the **back swing** and
through swing are restricted
movements producing at best
a 75% swing. The stance,
back swing and through
swing show how the spine
has rotated on its **angle
of tilt**. This is also
fundamental
for even-surfaced
golf shots.

ANGLE OF ATTACK

Your **swing plane**, or angle of attack,
is severely limited by the contour of
the ground which, in this situation,
slopes away, and by the distance of
the ball which is greater than usual
from your **address** position. The
restrictions on the **take away** are
clearly visible (below left).

• ARMS
The arms swing the club up sharply and
steeply, and the **swing plane** – the line
which runs from your left wrist to the
elbow – points to the ball.

LOWER SUPPORT •
In the full **take away** you
feel the strain on the
backs of the legs
increase, while your
buttocks help
maintain a counter-
balancing effect.
Keep the knees
flexed at an angle
and endeavour to
keep as low a
centre of gravity
as possible. To
rise up now
would ruin
your shot.

FOOT SUPPORT •
Secure as firm a foothold as
possible. This is where spiked
soles are so valuable (see p.18).
Any "footloose" movement
now, and you might take a
tumble. Try to feel heavy
but relaxed – as though the
ground were coming up
through your feet.

THROUGH SWING
As with the ball above stance shot,
the forward swing, hit and **follow
through** bring instant relief to the
discomfort of posture, **back swing**
and balance.

SKILL

10

PLAYING THE GAME

Definition: *Putting into practice all the weekend skills*

WITHIN YOUR OWN CAPABILITIES – and limitations – aim to avoid the various traps and hazards designed by the golf course architect. Concentrate on the immediate target rather than on the golf swing.

OBJECTIVE: To negotiate the ball from the teeing ground to the hole in as few shots as possible. *Rating* •••

APPROACH WITH CAUTION

A par-4 hole of 370m (420yd) with a bird's-eye view of the hazards and obstacles to be avoided.

Recommended route for beginners

Direct route for professionals

• TEEING OFF
Ladies from red markers (front); men from yellow (middle); competition from white tees (back).

• FAIRWAY
The **fairway** is the area of mown grass from where your second and third shots are (hopefully) played. Shots landing in longer grass off the fairway are in the **rough**.

• OUT OF BOUNDS
White stakes often mark the **boundary** line of the course. You must replay any ball which crosses this line – from the position where the last shot was played, and add a penalty stroke.

• ROUTE PLANNER
The blue line from tee to hole is the beginner's route.

• FRINGE
The **fringe** or **apron** is the area surrounding the **green** – up to 4m (13ft) from the putting surface.

• GREEN
The **green** is the area where the grass is cut shortest allowing a smooth, and sometimes very fast, roll of the ball. Use only a putter on this surface.

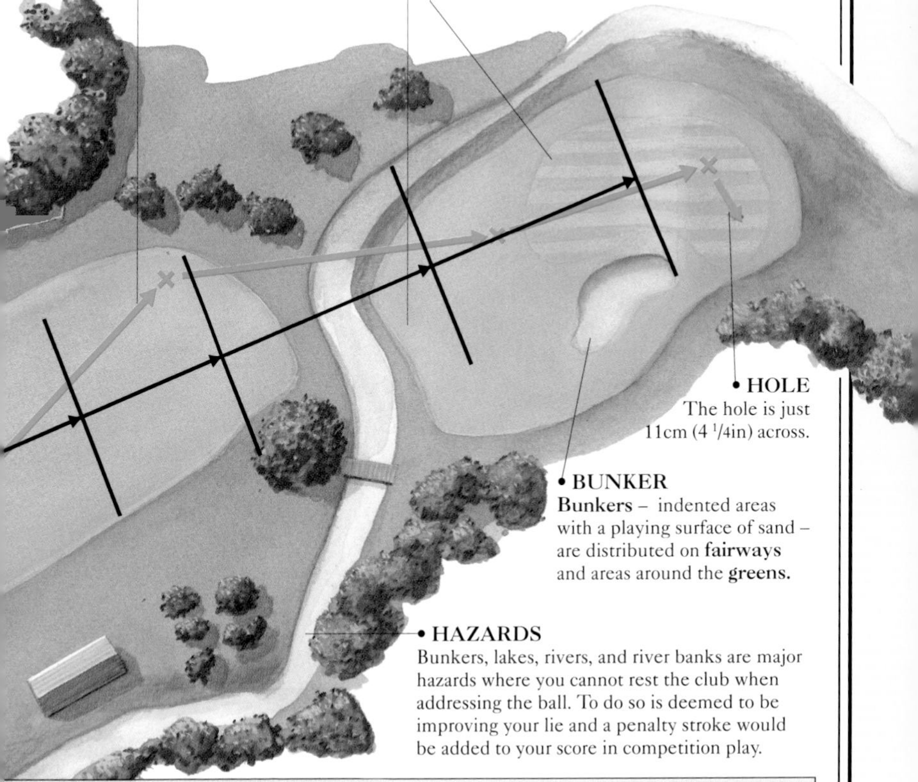

• HOLE
The hole is just 11cm (4 1/4in) across.

• BUNKER
Bunkers – indented areas with a playing surface of sand – are distributed on **fairways** and areas around the **greens.**

• HAZARDS
Bunkers, lakes, rivers, and river banks are major hazards where you cannot rest the club when addressing the ball. To do so is deemed to be improving your lie and a penalty stroke would be added to your score in competition play.

PERCENTAGE PLAY

POINTERS TO POSITIVE PLAY
• The professional will hit the green in 2 shots, but until you have the pro's power and control of the ball, take the safe route avoiding bunkers and trees as shown above. Play within your capabilities.
• Give every shot a target and each hole a plan in terms of your own playing ability. Good golf shots begin with a good set-up, so set yourself up to a specific target.
• Get **target-orientated**. You can't hit good golf shots by thinking about "how to swing the club". Visualize the hit ball landing in your target zone successfully.

DON'T THINK AHEAD
• Think in the present tense, and play one shot at a time, dealing with just that shot. Worry about the next shot later. You cannot play good golf shots if you are concerned about what lies ahead.
• Show respect for the golf course architect. He knows how you think. He presents challenges – but you don't have to take them on.
• Pars are for pros – they're expected to reach the green of a par-3 hole in 1 shot, a par-4 hole in 2, and a par-5 hole in 3 shots. You are not playing badly if you can't.

SKILL

10

• OUT OF BOUNDS
The white fence indicates out of bounds. If you hit into this area you must replay the shot and add a penalty stroke. Avoid this by teeing up as near to the hazard as the **markers** allow: you will aim naturally to a safe part of the **fairway**.

TEEING OFF

Before teeing off visualize the ball landing in the target area. See it fly as you want it to, and see yourself playing the shot well. Visualize yourself from the target playing the shot well, avoiding the out of bounds.

No. 7
YDS
MTRS
PAI

No. 12
YDS 407
MTRS 372
PAR 4
S.I. 10

DISTANCE PLATES
Usually positioned by the tee markers, distance markers tell you at a glance the hole number, length in yards and metres, par number and **stroke index** (see pp.88-89) and help you to plan your strategy for the hole as well as your teeing-off drive.

TEEING OFF TIPS

VARY THE TEE
Use a **tee peg** when teeing off because the ball is being swept away on the up swing. A tee helps you get sufficient loft from the least-lofted clubs such as the driver. Use a long or short tee as necessary so that half the ball shows above the top of the **wood**.

DRIVING DOWNWIND
Facing downwind leave the **driver** in your bag and tee off with a more **lofted wood** such as a No 3 or 4. This gets the ball airborne more quickly, allowing the force of the wind to carry the ball down the **fairway**. You will send the ball further this way. Use a tee, but be careful not to place it too high in the ground.

UPWIND
Don't attempt to hit the ball harder into the wind – but instead try to hit it better. Think along the lines of: "into a breeze swing with ease". Windy conditions can affect your rhythm so focus on a good relaxed set up and a rhythmical swing.

YOUR SECOND SHOT

SAFETY STRATEGY •
Always look for a safe alternative approach to avoid going directly over an obstacle or hazard. Plan a specific target for each shot that steers you clear of potential trouble.

It's far better to play short of the river than to gamble and risk everything by trying to clear it and the tree from here. Remember, in this situation the direct route (shown here in grey) is risky, while the alternative route (shown here in blue) is more sensible for the beginner.

• IDEAL APPROACH
The ideal shot for the inexperienced player is one of about 110m (120yd) to the left of the tree. This puts you in a good position for a simple approach to the putting surface.

• MISHITS
Don't be frightened of making mistakes. Mishits happen, so the secret of golf is to deal with one shot at a time and deal with the next one later.

AVOID GAMBLING
If you are forced to play directly away from the flag, think of it as a loan to the course that you can call in later.

THE CLUB FACE GAME

LOW-FLYING PITCH
If you have hit an errant shot simply get the ball back into play, even if it means playing sideways or backwards. Here the ball is lying in the longer grass stymied by the tree, and the best option is to play it out sideways avoiding the over-hanging branches. However, as your skills improve, your options will be more than just pitching out to the side. Taking a 9-iron or wedge you could play a punch-like shot direct to the flag, keeping the club head low to the target. With your weight also more on the left side at the swing you'll be able to impart some back spin to stop it from rolling over the green and down the bank. But it will still run further than a high pitch.

SKILL
10 ACROSS THE RIVER

You have to cross the river so use a **lofted** 8- or 9-iron to carry the ball safely over. It's best to play to the front part of the **green** and avoid the **bunker**, or even short of it.

PLAN EACH SHOT
From this position of roughly 110m (120yd) to the hole, aim to **hole out** in no more than 3 shots.

• COMING IN TO LAND
Although the plan is to hit the **green**, the slight mishit will be safe enough on the front **fringe**.

ROUGH TREATMENT

BALL IN LONG GRASS
If you accidentally alter the ball's position, at the **address**, it is counted as a stroke. If the ball is sitting reasonably in the longer grass use the same method as when playing a **bunker** shot (see pp.65-67) with the **club face** looking at your target and your body **alignment** slightly open (aiming left).

BALL DEEP IN LONG GRASS
If the ball sits in the roots of long grass, hold the lofted club firmly and play the shot powerfully with the ball back in the stance. Use an early wrist break and take a steep upward and downward swing of the arms, while the right knee remains flexed, and the head stays still.

BALL IN TROUBLE
Never imagine the shot you have to play as a threat to your ego or your confidence – because you will respond to it in a nervous, inhibited fashion. See each shot as an opportunity to recover from the situation. Never attempt to play a shot until you are clear about what you want the ball to do. Picture where you want the ball to land, and how you want the ball to fly or roll, remembering that it is the **club face**, not you, that hits the ball.

CHIPPING CLUB
A putt with a 7-iron lofts the ball on to the putting surface and allows the ball to roll up to the hole.

IDEAL APPROACH •
Play the ball onto the lower level of the **green** shown here and let the ball run up the slope. Don't flight the ball to the plateau of the green. It might not stop in time and would then run down the bank into deep water and trouble.

CHIPPING ON TO THE GREEN

The hole is at the back of the tiered **green** and there is a steep bank behind down to the river. The pitch was not perfect but it has finished safely on the **fringe** of the green and now you need to "putt with a lofted **putter**".

HOLING OUT

Your chip shot rolls up to within 1m (3ft) of the hole. Now it's time for the short putt to **hole out**. Don't be careless with this final shot. The game can be won or lost with the putt, and this shot has the same stroke value as a drive of over 180m (200yd).

MENTAL APPROACH
Expect to hole it. Negative thoughts, doubts and uncertainties cause your stroke to be tentative and you will miss. Imagine and stick to your chosen line, and make your stroke positive, remembering that authority of contact comes from one third on the **back swing** and two thirds on the **through swing**.

• AIMING
Even on heavily contoured **greens** every putt is a straight putt – straight, that is, to a point from which the ball will be taken by the slope.

• PUTT FIRMLY
Putts that are short don't go in, so try not to mishit the short putts. Strike them firmly enough to go 15cm (6in) beyond the hole – should you miss it.

AFTER THE WEEKEND

Taking your techniques on to the golf course

NOW YOU HAVE COMPLETED the weekend course you should think about joining a club if you really wish to progress further. At the golf club you will have access to a pro, a shop with a wide range of golf equipment (including second-hand clubs), a practice area, often a driving range as well, and the chance to play with partners at your level and better. Make enquiries at private clubs in your area. As they limit the size of membership it is possible that the club you want to join will have a waiting list. Contact the club manager, or secretary, asking for an application for membership. You will need to pay an entrance fee and an annual subscription.

How to get a handicap

Many clubs insist that potential members have an official handicap (see pp.88-89) before applications are considered. This is a Catch 22 situation as you must first be a member of a club before you can achieve an official handicap. There are, however, public golf courses where golfers pay as they play, and most do have a membership section where you can apply for a handicap. Understandably, they are busier than private clubs, but these courses are good training grounds, allowing you to gain the experience in playing the game.

Meaningful practice

Whether you play at a private or public course, think about top-up instruction from a professional, perhaps a 30 minute lesson once a month. You don't have to be a member of the pro's club in order to have lessons. You only get out of golf what you put in.

PRACTICE PLAY

Aiming to get on target mentally and physically

YOU COULD SPEND ANOTHER WEEKEND on just how and what to practise, but there are key pointers to consider. **1** You must practise regularly. **2** Keep practice sessions short. Six 30-minute sessions a week are more meaningful and beneficial than one three-hour session once a week. **3** Be clear about what you are going to practise. Simply to hit golf balls achieves nothing. **4** Split each practice session into three equal parts to avoid becoming bored.

TARGET PRACTICE

Chip plastic air-flow balls into an open umbrella for target practice. Try it with your eyes closed because when you remove the vision you remove your judgement and other senses come into play – senses of feel, balance, rhythm and ease of movement. Once you are clear about what is required your confidence grows.

PRESSURE
Set yourself a target of 20 shots and, if you miss, start again. When you get to shot 15, start counting down aloud to put pressure on yourself to finish the practice successfully.

ENERGY FORCES
Avoid trying too hard to get it right by thinking about every move. Trust your kinetic senses – your senses of motion and energy. They won't be far out and will even self-correct for a more successful result next time if you trust them. First lob a few balls underarm into the umbrella, then apply the same feel when using the club.

SWING NATURALLY

Feel the movement coming from the rotation of the body rather than from a pick-up of the arm. The body rotates as the arms swing up and then rotates again as the arms swing down.

CHANGE HANDS
Swing the club first with the right arm, then with the left. This will help you get to know the feel of the swing. Doing this with each arm individually builds up good muscle memory as well as good club control.

TYRE TESTING
A good swing carries force, so get to feel the correct order of the forward swing: first the body rotating, then the arms swinging down, and, lastly the **club head** lagging behind. Practise hitting against an old car tyre to help you to sense the effortless power of this action.

GOLF – THE INNER GAME

MIND GAME
• When your mind can perceive it, your body can achieve it – but not until then. Visualize clearly what it is that you want your body to do then let it happen.
• Any physical movement induced by conscious thought becomes inefficient. Think about this. Even walking becomes difficult the more you think about how to do it. So just put one foot in front of the other and keep moving.
• Be mindful not thoughtful during every level and phase of your practice. Being mindful is being aware of things as they are – the physical sensation of rhythm and balance; of smoothness of movement; of weight transfer and effortless interactions. To be thoughtful is to think about doing each movement which then becomes awkward.
• Practising on a putting green and driving range is fine, provided you are not merely hitting balls, one after the other.

PRACTICE PUTTING GREEN
Over half your shots on a golf course will be putts – so keep up the target practice using the practice greens that golf clubs provide.

HOW TO SCORE

Understanding handicaps and basic scoring methods

AT THIS STAGE YOU NEED ONLY CONCERN yourself with two basic methods of scoring in golf: the medal system (also known as strokeplay), and the **Stableford** system. Many alternative games can be played but these are generally variants of Stableford or medal play. The medal system is the game that is almost always played in professional golf. However, most beginners prefer Stableford because, whereas in the medal system one bad hole can ruin your entire score for the round, the Stableford method has the advantage of being a points per hole system (see opposite page). The scorecards may seem complicated at first, but once you become familiar with some of the scoring terms – the most important of which are outlined over these pages – you should have no difficulties.

THE HANDICAP SYSTEM

EQUAL OPPORTUNITIES

The **handicap** system is designed to allow golfers of various levels of ability and experience to compete on level terms.

• A handicap represents a number of shots allowed to a player above par for the course – that is, the number of strokes a professional is expected to take to complete all the holes (see opposite).

• A good amateur may play off a handicap of 9, for example, which means that for each of the 9 most difficult holes, indicated by the **stroke index** (see opposite), the player receives an extra shot, playing to par for the rest of the course.

• In strokeplay, where the emphasis is on the total number of strokes required to complete the course, a player's handicap can simply be deducted from his **gross score** to find the nett total (final score). In other scoring systems you may be allowed to take advantage of only a percentage of your handicap, for example, only 7/8th is permitted for the **Stableford** system.

KNOW YOUR HANDICAP

• A man who is taking up golf can expect a maximum 28 handicap, or lower, allowing for an extra shot on every hole and 10 more besides. Those 10 extra strokes will again be designated to the 10 most difficult holes indicated by the stroke index. A lady novice may expect a 36 or lower handicap – 2 extra strokes for every hole.

• The system may at first seem generous enough. Once out on the course, however, you may find that there is a great deal more than 28/36 strokes' difference between your own score and that of a golfer who plays off **scratch** (without a handicap). Don't be too disheartened; rather, look forward to the sense of achievement you will feel the first time that you "play to your handicap".

• If you join a new club you have to re-establish your handicap. This will be calculated from the average score of 3 games, played over the same course with a player who already possesses a handicap.

STABLEFORD

In the Stableford system if you have a bad hole, where you have played 2 shots more than your nett par, you forfeit the chance for points at that hole and simply pick up the ball and hope to do better at the next. If you manage to play the hole to just 1 over your nett par, then you are awarded 1 point. If you play to nett par for the hole, you are awarded 2 points; for 1 under, 3 points, and for 2 under, 4 points. The player scoring the most points for the 18 holes is declared the winner.

SCORE CARD

Swop cards and mark each other's scores in the "A" column. Mark your own score in the "marker" column on the left. At the end of play each of the players checks and signs the cards.

MEDAL (OR STROKEPLAY)

In medal or strokeplay, the number of shots taken at each hole is entered on to the score card in the appropriate box then totalled for the 18 holes to obtain the **gross score**. The player's full handicap is then deducted to determine the nett score for the round.

STABLEFORD card

COMPETITION	STABLEFORD					
	S.S.S. DATE 21-7-90	H/CAP 24	STROKES RECEIVED 21

TEE		S.S.S.	
WHITE	72	71	PLAYER A. K. RYAN
YELLOW	72	70	PLAYER B.
RED	74	74	

(Stableford scorecard, signed "M. Lunn", MARKER'S SIGNATURE / PLAYER'S SIGNATURE)

MEDAL card

COMPETITION	MEDAL			DATE 19-8-90		

TEE		S.S.S.			H/CAP	STROKES RECEIVED
WHITE	72	71	PLAYER A. J. HARRISON		21	
YELLOW	72	70	PLAYER B.			
RED	74	74				

MARKER	PARTNER	HOLE	YARDS	PAR	YARDS	PAR	STROKE INDEX	A	PTS	B	PTS	YARDS	PAR	STROKE INDEX
6		1	524	5	504	5	15	6				461	5	13
5		2	365	4	355	4	11	4				336	4	5
6		3	426	4	414	4	1	7				426	5	3
5		4	195	3	170	3	5	4				165	3	15
5		5	444	4	432	4	7	4				358	4	11
5		6	391	4	376	4	9	5				361	4	1
4		7	137	3	135	3	17	4				137	3	17
6		8	548	5	536	5	13	4				450	5	9
5		9	413	4	398	4	3	5				383	5	7
47			3443	36	3320	36	TOTAL OUT	49				3077	38	
5		10	317	4	300	4	8	4				259	4	10
6		11	500	5	485	5	14	6				468	5	6
5		12	414	4	399	4	4	5				379	4	4
4		13	139	3	130	3	18	3				115	3	18
5		14	381	4	360	4	10	5				350	4	2
5		15	403	4	386	4	2	4				376	5	12
5		16	346	4	341	4	16	4				312	4	16
5		17	165	3	160	3	6	4				140	3	14
6		18	362	4	360	4	12	5				337	4	8
46			3027	35	2921	35	TOTAL IN	43				2736	36	
93			6470	71	6241	71	TOTAL	92				5813	74	
22							H'CAP	21						
71							NETT	71						

MARKER'S SIGNATURE *M. Lunn*   PLAYER'S SIGNATURE *James Harrison*

PAR •

Par represents the number of strokes a professional is expected to take at each hole. Assuming 2 putts per **green**, he should take 1 shot to reach a Par 3 – up to 270m (250yd) in length; 2 shots at Par 4 – 270-508m (251-475yd); and 3 at a Par 5 – over 508m (476yd). The total of all the pars equals Par for the course.

TOTALS •

Under column "A" the player's score has been recorded as 49 for the 9 outward holes and 43 for the 9 inward, totalling 92 gross. On deducting the 21 **handicap**, the final score is 71.

STROKE INDEX •

The **stroke index** indicates the difficulty of each hole. The number 1 represents the most difficult; 18 is the easiest. The men's stroke index is based on distance, the ladies' more on individual difficulty.

PLAY BY THE RULES

A beginner's guide to essential rules and etiquette

THE RULES OF THE GAME, formalized by the Royal & Ancient Golf Club of St Andrews, Scotland, and the US Golf Association, cover competition play, including club and ball specifications, throughout the world. At club level, you will encounter local rules as they affect out of bounds areas, special course hazards and seasonal variations. But your chief concern should be with golf etiquette – that is, good on-course behaviour and how it affects other golfers. It may be a matter of common sense and good manners, but it needs to be mastered, just like the game itself does.

FLAG TENDING

Only from long range will an opponent request that you tend the flag. This occurs when he cannot see the hole. Hold the flag standing down shadow of it and remove it as the ball draws near. Never throw the flag down or drop it casually. Lay it on the ground carefully out of the way of play.

STAND CLEAR •
Tend the flag clear of the hole and don't stand on another player's line.

THE GREEN CODE •
Generally, you may not putt with the flag in the hole – except when you are standing off the putting surface.

MARKING THE BALL

In competition play a player may ask you to mark your ball if it obstructs his line to the hole. Place a **marker** or coin behind the ball and remove the ball. Until you start to play in competitons, keep play moving and hole out.

• THINK OF OTHERS
Be careful not to affect the line of putt of other players.

SLOW PLAY
Avoid slow play. Inexperienced players will naturally take more shots, and more time, so keep putting until you hole out.

PUTT PROCEDURE •
In competition play if you putt and miss the hole, you may continue putting to hole out, or mark your ball.

FLAG DOWN •
Leave the flag well away from the hole and always replace it afterwards.

COURSE COMPANION

ESSENTIAL ETIQUETTE
• Replace your divots;tread them in firmly.
• Rake the bunker before you leave it.
• Repair your pitchmarks on the greens. Unless repaired immediately they can take weeks to recover.
• Never take your trolley or bag on to **teeing grounds** or putting **greens**.
• Always keep a clear distance from your playing partner – preferably so he knows where you are.
• Stand quietly when your playing partner is about to play a shot.
• Shout **"fore"** loudly if you think your ball may hit another player.
• Do not play your own shot until the players ahead of you are out of range.
• Invite players behind to play through if you're taking time.

The correct way to drop a ball that is unplayable is to let it go at arm's length – not over your shoulder.

SLOW PLAY
• Don't rush your shot but walk quickly between each one. Beginners are welcomed by everyone when they are seen to be keeping their place on the course.
• Don't spectate – anticipate. Always be ready to play your own shot especially on the greens.
• Keep moving forwards. If you are playing from the front fringe of the green, first take your bag or trolley to the exit part of the green then return to your ball with your putter and whichever other club is required for the shot. Having **holed out** you can then leave the green immediately.
•Never mark your scorecard on the putting green. Do this on the next **teeing ground**.
• If in doubt, consult your playing partner first.

GLOSSARY

A

•**Address** Your start position
•**Alignment (body)** The direction in which the lines across the toes, hips and shoulders point when you are standing at address.
•**Alignment (club face)** The direction in which the club face looks or faces, either at address or at impact.
•**Angle of tilt** The angle of the spine and upper body in the address position.

B

•**Back spin** The reverse spin of the ball imparted by one of the more lofted, shorter, clubs.
•**Back swing** The start of the swing movement.
•**Birdie** A score of 1 shot less than par for the hole.
•**Bite** A ball that stops quickly after landing on the green.
•**Blade** The term used to describe a traditional design of iron.
•**Bogey** A score of 1 over par for the hole.
•**Bottom edge** The leading edge of the iron which sits on the ground.
•**Boundary** The outer limit of the golf course.
•**Bunker** Termed as a hazard: a sand filled hollow on fairways and around greens.
•**Butt** The tip of the golf club handle.

C

•**Cavity backed** A term given to a design of iron – best for beginners.
•**Closed stance** Where a right handed

golfer aligns himself right of the target.
•**Club face** The flat area of the golf club head designed to strike the ball.
•**Club head** The head of the wood or iron as opposed to the shaft or grip.
•**Compression** Term representing the density of a golf ball.

D

•**Dimples** Indentations on golf balls determining the aerodynamics.
•**Driver** The longest and least lofted club used from the teeing ground to commence a long hole.

E

•**Eagle** A score which is 2 under par for the hole.

F

•**Fairway** The area of mown grass between the tee and the green.
•**Flight** Term to describe the behaviour of the ball when airborne.
•**Follow through** The completion of the swing after contacting the ball.
•**"Fore"** A cry of warning that an errant shot is coming your way.
•**Fringe or apron** The border of the green.

G

•**Green** That area of finely mown grass where golfers putt to hole out.
•**Grooves** The score-lines on the hitting surface of the wood or iron.
•**Gross score** The total number of shots made over 18 holes.

H

•**Handicap** An equalizing system. It is awarded in the first instance based on an average between the player's gross score and the par for the course.
•**Heel** The club face below the shaft.
•**Hole out** To complete the hole by putting into the cup on the green.
•**Hook** A ball which for the right handed player moves in a curve from right to left in the air.

L

•**Loft** The angle of the flat hitting surface of the club face.

M

•**Marker** A person who records your score in competition play; or any object used to identify the precise position of the ball on the putting green when it has been lifted for cleaning.

O

•**Open stance** Where the right handed player aligns himself left of the target.

P

•**Posture** The pose one adopts when standing over the ball.
•**Primary target** Anything on the ground approximately one metre in front of the ball but in line with the ultimate target, for easier alignment of club face.
•**Putter** The club used for holing out.

R

•**Rough** Areas of longer grass which border each fairway and green.

S

•**Sand wedge** The lofted club that is used for playing shots out of bunkers.
•**Scratch** To equal par of the course. A scratch golfer has a zero handicap.
•**Scuffed** When the club hits the ground before hitting the ball.
•**Shaft** The rod connecting the handle to the club head.
•**Slice** A shot which for the right handed player bends from left to right in the air.
•**Sole** That part of the club which rests on the ground.
•**Solid** Term given to the type of golf ball which is either of 1 piece or 2, having a large inner-core and thick outer cover. Also a term to describe the feel of perfect contact on the ball.
•**Spin** The way the ball rotates.
•**Spikes** Studs in the soles of golf shoes.
•**Square** Facing (club face) or in line with (body) the target.
•**Stableford** A points scoring system.
•**Stance** The position the player adopts when addressing the ball.

•**Standard scratch score** The score based on the degree of difficulty of a particular course.
•**Stroke** A shot played. Even an air shot (one missed completely) counts if the ball has been addressed properly.
•**Stroke index** An indicator to show the degree of difficulty of each hole and to show where shots are awarded in matchplay dependent on handicaps.
•**Sweet spot** That part of the club face which produces perfect contact.
•**Swing path** The direction in which the club head travels through impact.
•**Swing plane** The angle of arc away from and into the ball.

T

•**Take away** The first move of the backward swing.
•**Target line** An imaginary line from the ball directly to the target.
•**Target orientating** Tuning your mind and body to the target.
•**Tee peg** Support for the ball used on the teeing ground.
•**Teeing ground** The starting point for each hole.
•**Tempo** The speed of the swing.
•**Thin** A shot on the upswing which shoots along the ground to the right.
•**Through swing** That part of the swing just after contact with the ball.
•**Trajectory** The flight of the ball on take-off.

V

• **Vardon grip** The text-book method of holding the club.

W

• **Wood** A type of club used for long range shots. The club head may be made of wood or metal.

INDEX

GETTING IN TOUCH

Royal & Ancient Golf Club of St. Andrews, Fife, Scotland	Professional Golfers Association Apollo House, The Belfry, Sutton Coldfield, West Midlands B76 9PT	English Golf Union, 1-3 Upper King St., Leicester, LE1 6XF.

ACKNOWLEDGMENTS

Peter Ballingall and Dorling Kindersley would like to thank the following for their contribution and support in the production of this book:

Barnham Broom Golf & Country Club, Norwich, Norfolk NR9 4DD (tel. 01603 759393), and Stephen Beckham, the Club Professional, for the loan of golf clothes and accessories.
Ross McCue for his modelling and expertise.
Joanna Turner for her modelling, time and patience.
Mrs R.L. Harrison, Administration Manager at Mizuno (UK) Ltd, Imperial Way, Worton Grange, Reading, Berks. RG2 OTD for the loan of the golf clubs and bags.
Acushnet (UK) Ltd, Caxton Road, St Ives Industrial Estate, St Ives, Huntingdon, Cambs. PE17 4LS for golf balls and transparencies.
The Golf Ball (a very handy booklet covering the technical story of the golf ball) is available from Acushnet /Titleist on receipt of a S.A.E.
Gilbert Lloyd and Peter Gregory at Richmond Golf Club, for help with golf flags, poles, cups and markers and location shooting.

Philip Gatward for the location photography. Plough Studios, Clapham, London for indoor photography space and London Workshop for the high-speed flash.
Paul Bailey for the full-colour illustrations. Janos Marffy, Rob Shone, Craig Austin and Paul Wilding for line drawings. Tracy Hambleton and Kevin Williams for design assistance.